STAR WARS

WORKBOOKS

3RD GRADE READING AND WRITING

FOR AGES 8–9

BY THE EDITORS OF BRAIN QUEST
CONSULTING EDITOR: BARBARA BLACK

WORKMAN PUBLISHING
NEW YORK

BRAIN QUEST and WORKMAN are registered trademarks of Workman Publishing Co., Inc.

Library of Congress Cataloging-in-Publication Data is available.

ISBN 978-0-7611-8938-1

Workbook series designer Raquel Jaramillo
Designers Tim Hall, Abby Dening
Writers Bridget Heos, Megan Butler
Editors Nathalie Le Du, Olivia Swomley, Zoe Maffitt
Production Editor Jessica Rozler
Production Manager Julie Primavera

Workman books are available at special discounts when purchased in bulk for premiums and sales promotions as well as for fund-raising or educational use. Special editions or book excerpts can also be created to specification. For details, contact the Special Sales Director at the address below, or send an e-mail to specialmarkets@workman.com.

Workman Publishing Co., Inc.
225 Varick Street
New York, NY 10014-4381

workman.com
starwars.com
starwarsworkbooks.com

Printed in the United States of America

First printing November 2017

10 9 8 7 6 5 4 3 2

STAR WARS
WORKBOOKS

This workbook belongs to:

_____

Re-create Words

When a **prefix** is added to a root word, it changes the meaning of the root word.

Draw a line to match each prefix to a root word.

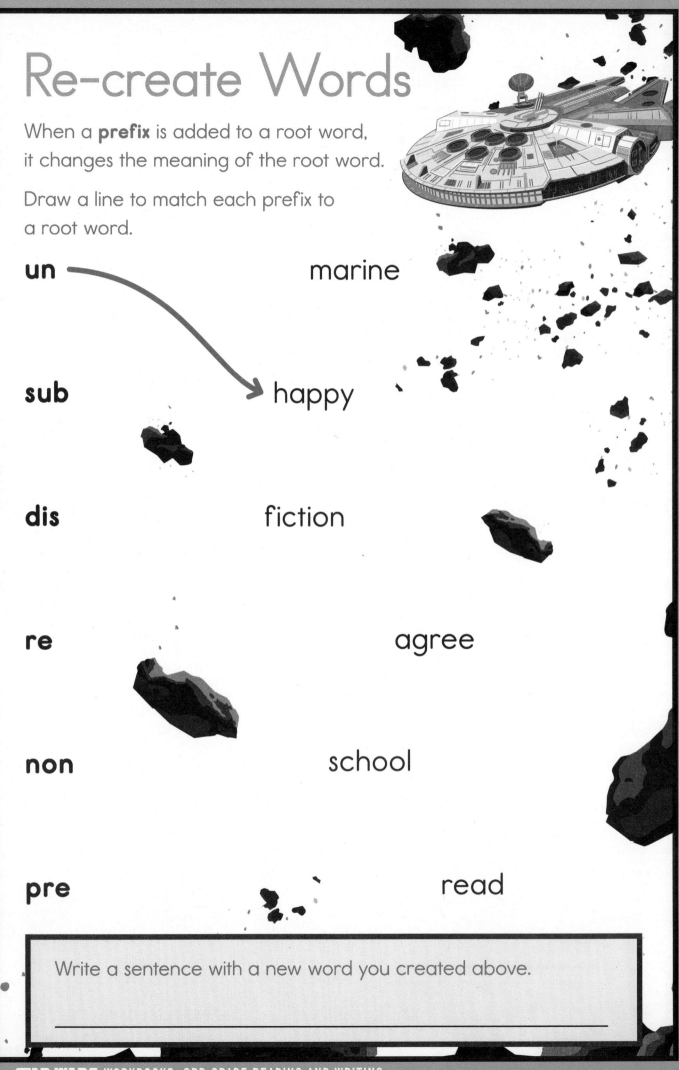

un   marine

sub   happy

dis   fiction

re   agree

non   school

pre   read

Write a sentence with a new word you created above.

_____

Incomplete Words

Draw a line to match each **prefix** to a root word.
Then write each new word below.

literate

in

correct

possible

il

complete

legal

im

perfect

appropriate

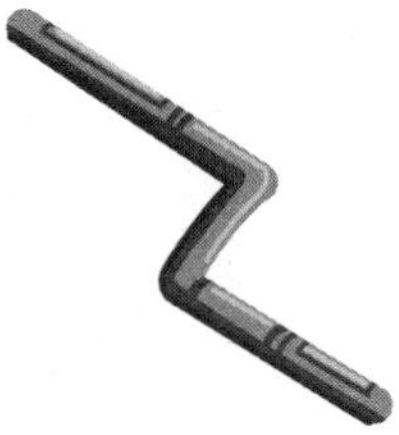

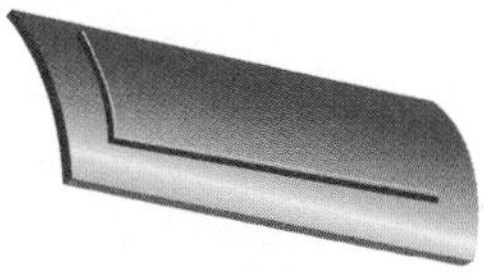

illiterate

_____   _____

_____   _____

_____

_____

_____

Resisting Bravely

A **suffix** is added to the end of a root word to change its meaning. Read the definition and example for each suffix. Then write the correct word with its suffix for each definition.

-y
having
chill ⌐
chilly

-ness
state of being
happy ⌐
happiness

-able
can be done
understand ⌐
understandable

-ly
in this way
quick ⌐
quickly

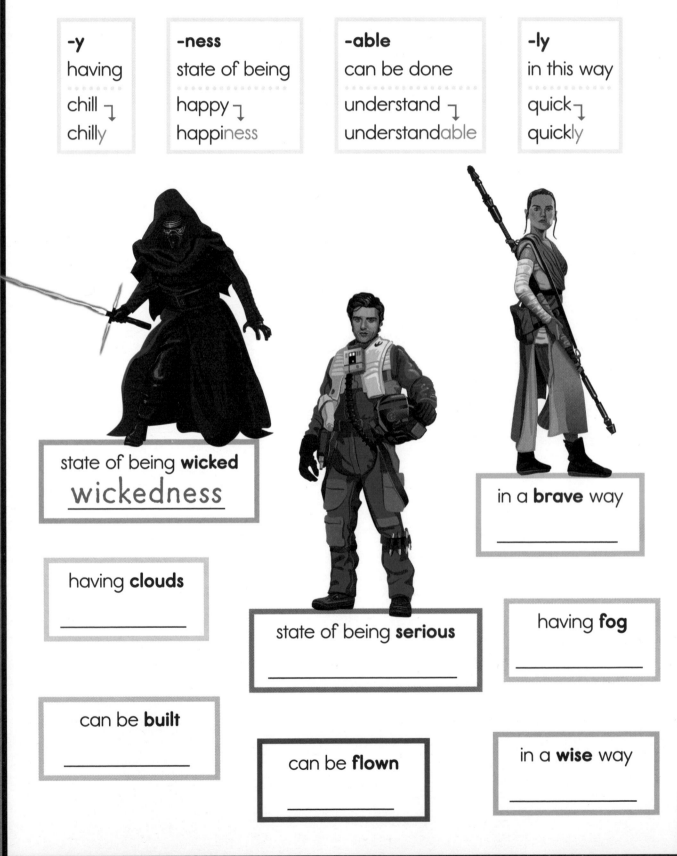

state of being **wicked**
wickedness

in a **brave** way
_____

having **clouds**
_____

state of being **serious**
_____

having **fog**
_____

can be **built**
_____

can be **flown**
_____

in a **wise** way
_____

Wordy Droids

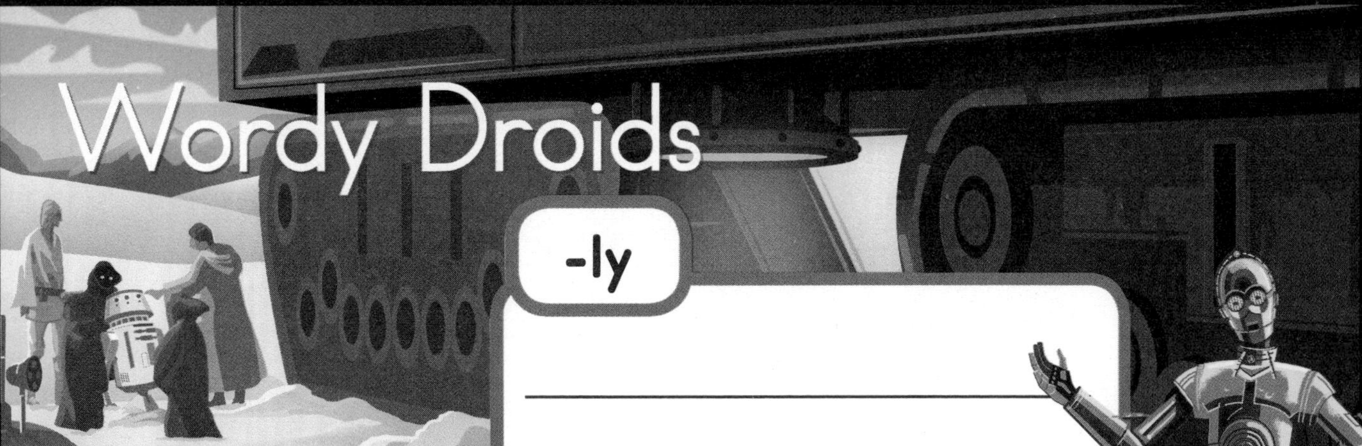

Write four words you know that contain each **suffix**.

-ly

_____

_____

_____

_____

-y

_____

_____

_____

-ness

_____

_____

_____

-able

_____

_____

_____

Decode Words

Circle the root word. Then add the **prefix** or **suffix** to it. Write the new word two times.

(swamp) + y   swampy   swampy

in + put   _____   _____

orbit + ing   _____   _____

dis + trust   _____   _____

fight + er   _____   _____

pre + plan   _____   _____

hope + ful   _____   _____

tele + scope   _____   _____

farm + er   _____   _____

dis + able   _____   _____

Scavenger Rey

Underline the **prefix** or **suffix** of each word below. Then find the words in the word search.

helpful   fearless   dishonest   unknown

rebuild   defender   forceful   mislead

U	M	S	W	B	I	C	L	G	V	V	D
N	N	J	G	D	U	U	E	O	I	I	B
K	X	T	Y	D	F	O	R	Y	S	F	K
N	G	B	D	E	M	W	C	H	C	V	O
O	O	D	U	C	A	N	P	O	U	N	M	I
W	B	R	U	R	E	N	W	E	M	T	D
N	O	L	S	S	E	L	R	A	E	F	L
F	R	V	Q	S	O	L	S	V	Y	J	I
I	P	O	T	V	M	X	N	I	N	Q	U
H	E	L	P	F	U	L	Z	C	M	Q	B
R	E	D	N	E	F	E	D	W	G	D	E
V	S	M	H	J	O	X	K	Z	Z	S	R

Write the words in alphabetical order.

_____

_____

_____

Deserted in the Desert

Homographs are words that are spelled alike but mean different things. They may also have different pronunciations.

Choose the correct meaning for each homograph.

Luke lived in the **desert** of Tatooine.

- ☑ a. desert (noun): an ecosystem with little rainfall
- ☐ b. desert (verb): to leave someone behind who needs help

Padmé's royal demeanor and style **entrance** the people of Naboo.

- ☐ a. entrance (noun): the place where one enters or exits
- ☐ b. entrance (verb): to hold one's attention or to fill with wonder

Watto **moped** after losing his slave Anakin in a bet.

- ☐ a. moped (verb): acted sad and hopeless
- ☐ b. moped (noun): a small motorcycle

In most cases, Bail Organa will **object** to war.

- ☐ a. object (noun): something that can be seen or touched
- ☐ b. object (verb): to state one's disagreement

The rebels had a **minute** chance of escaping the Death Star.

- ☐ a. minute (noun): the period of time that takes up 60 seconds
- ☐ b. minute (adjective): very small

As Finn trekked across the snow, his toes grew **number**.

- ☐ a. number (noun): a word or symbol representing a certain amount
- ☐ b. number (adjective): more numb

Write a sentence that includes each homograph, using either meaning.

desert

_____

entrance

_____

moped

_____

object

_____

minute

_____

number

_____

Capital City

A **noun** describes a person, place, or thing.
Proper nouns name specific people, places, and things and begin with a capital letter.

Circle the proper noun in each pair.
Rewrite it with correct capitalization.

planet	(lothal)	_Lothal_
warrior	ahsoka tano	_____
r2-d2	droid	_____
cad bane	bounty hunter	_____
leader	count dooku	_____
chewbacca	copilot	_____
teacher	obi-wan kenobi	_____
hero	anakin skywalker	_____
captain rex	clone trooper	_____

A **title** is a word or words that describe a person's job. Titles appear before a person's name. They begin with a capital letter.

Rewrite each sentence using correct capitalization for titles and other proper nouns.

padmé was elected queen amidala at age fourteen.

Padmé was elected Queen Amidala at age fourteen.

anakin skywalker met padmé when she was disguised as a handmaiden.

_____

At the time, anakin and his mother, shmi, were slaves on tatooine.

_____

Later, anakin and padmé got married.

_____

r2-d2 and c-3po were wedding guests.

_____

padmé had twins, luke and leia.

_____

luke and leia were hidden from emperor palpatine.

_____

luke skywalker was raised by his aunt and uncle on tatooine.

_____

Like Luke

The words below have the same vowel sound as **Luke**.

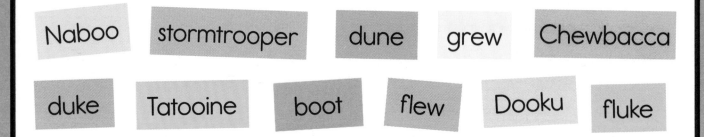

Naboo   stormtrooper   dune   grew   Chewbacca

duke   Tatooine   boot   flew   Dooku   fluke

Sort the words by spelling pattern in the boxes below.

ew

_____

_____

_____

oo

_____

_____

_____

_____

u_e

_____

_____

_____

Sentient Sentence

A sentence must end with a **period**, **question mark**, or **exclamation mark**. Add the correct punctuation mark to the end of each sentence.

Admiral Ackbar was a military commander for the Rebel Alliance

Did you know that he led major operations against the Empire

Ackbar planned a surprise attack on the second Death Star

Can you believe that he used construction plans collected by rebel spies

Ackbar worked with General Calrissian to lead the space battle

He led from his ship, the Mon Calamari cruiser *Home One*

When the battle did not go as planned, he shouted, "It's a trap "

Ackbar thought the troops needed to retreat right away

But General Calrissian convinced him to keep going

The rebels won and destroyed the Death Star

Roll the Credits

A **comma** is needed between items in a list, a city and state, and a date and year. Add commas where they are needed in each sentence.

George Lucas founded Lucasfilm in San Rafael California.

The first *Star Wars* movie was released May 25 1977.

It introduced the characters Luke Skywalker Princess Leia Han Solo and Chewbacca.

The movies in the first trilogy were *A New Hope The Empire Strikes Back* and *Return of the Jedi*.

The prequel trilogy included *The Phantom Menace Attack of the Clones* and *Revenge of the Sith*.

Lucasfilm headquarters are now in San Francisco California.

Star Wars: The Force Awakens was released December 18 2015.

New characters include Rey Finn Poe Kylo Ren and BB-8.

Settings include Takodana Starkiller Base and the desert planet Jakku.

Luke's Lightsaber

Possessive form shows that an item belongs to someone, something, or a group.

Write whose items appear in these pictures with the correct punctuation.

Chief Jawa

Chief Jawa's
ion blaster

Darth Vader

_____

_____

Tusken Raider

_____

_____

Greedo

_____

_____

Obi-Wan Kenobi

_____

_____

R5-D4

_____

_____

Luke

_____

_____

C-3PO and R2-D2 Visit Jabba the Hutt

When two or more characters are talking in a story, it's called **dialogue**. Quotation marks show that a character is talking. Commas are also used.

"Of course I'm worried. And you should be, too," C-3PO said to R2-D2.

Add the correct punctuation to C-3PO's dialogue with R2-D2. Then draw the scene.

R2-D2 and C-3PO stood at the door of the palace of Jabba the Hutt

Artoo are you sure this is the right place I better knock I suppose said C-3PO

C-3PO knocked then said There doesn't seem to be anyone there Let's go back and tell Master Luke

A small hatch in the door opened A large electronic eyeball popped out and looked at the two droids Then the hatch slammed shut

I don't think they're going to let us in Artoo We'd better go   said C-3PO as he turned to leave

The large door to the palace started to open with a loud screech The droids looked at each other afraid R2-D2 started to enter C-3PO rushed after him and the door lowered behind them

Artoo wait Oh dear Artoo Artoo I really don't think we should rush into all this   worried C-3PO

R2-D2 continued down the hallway with C-3PO following

C-3PO called after him Oh Artoo Artoo wait for me

Hutt History

A **past tense verb** describes an action that happened in the past. Fill in the blanks by changing each **verb** to the past tense.

The Hutts control the planet Tatooine.

The Hutts __controlled__ the planet Tatooine.

They smuggle illegal goods.

They _____ illegal goods.

Jabba the Hutt hires Han Solo and Chewbacca.

Jabba the Hutt _____ Han Solo and Chewbacca.

Darth Vader traps Han Solo in carbonite.

Darth Vader _____ Han Solo in carbonite.

Boba Fett delivers Han to Jabba the Hutt.

Boba Fett _____ Han to Jabba the Hutt.

Jabba places Han on the wall.

Jabba _____ Han on the wall.

Lando, Leia, and Chewbacca attempt to rescue him.

Lando, Leia, and Chewbacca _____ to rescue him.

Irregular verbs do not follow normal spelling rules when changing from present to past tense. Instead, the spelling may change completely or not at all.

Present: She is kind.	**Present:** They let him go.
Past: She was kind.	**Past:** They let him go.

Fill in the blanks by changing the irregular verb to the past tense.

Anakin and Shmi Skywalker are slaves of Gardulla the Hutt.

Anakin and Shmi Skywalker __were__ slaves of Gardulla the Hutt.

Anakin is angry at Gardulla the Hutt.

Anakin _____ angry at Gardulla the Hutt.

Gardulla loses a bet, so Watto becomes Anakin

and Shmi's new master.

Gardulla _____ a bet, so Watto _____

Anakin and Shmi's new master.

Watto sends Anakin to participate in a dangerous race.

Watto _____ Anakin to participate in a dangerous race.

Anakin speeds through the course and wins.

Anakin _____ through the course and _____ .

Anakin says good-bye to his mother.

Anakin _____ good-bye to his mother.

Anakin goes with the Jedi.

Anakin _____ with the Jedi.

Luke Looking Ahead

Imagine that you are a Jedi using the Force to see the future. Look at the pictures and write sentences about what will happen next in Luke's story. Write the verbs in **future tense**.

Luke <u>will talk to Yoda before he dies.</u>

Then, _____

_____

Next, _____

_____

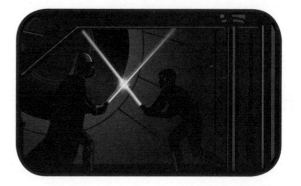

Afterward, _____

_____

Finally, _____

_____

Comparing Creatures and Aliens

Comparative adjectives compare two or more nouns.

Read the facts about the creatures. Circle the correct adjective or comparative adjective that completes the sentence.

Though both live in the desert, the bantha is **furry**/**furrier** than the eopie.

The Sarlacc is **hungry/ hungrier** than a Hutt.

The Gamorrean stands guard with **sharp/ sharper** teeth.

This **deadly/ deadlier** rancor belongs to Jabba the Hutt.

This Kowakian monkey-lizard laughs **long/longer** than the other creatures.

This **cute/cuter** Ortolan plays in the Max Rebo Band.

Fast, Faster, Fastest

Superlative adjectives compare three or more nouns and are adjectives that express the highest degree of something.

Han Solo believes the *Millennium Falcon* is the **fastest** ship in the galaxy.

Complete the chart, filling in the correct adjectives, comparative adjectives, and superlative adjectives.

adjective	comparative adjective	superlative adjective
tall	taller	tallest
	wiser	
dark		
	hungrier	
		rudest
	larger	
		fiercest
quick		
		cutest
	tinier	

Write a sentence about your favorite Jedi using a superlative adjective from the chart.

_____

_____

Describing Droids

Adverbs describe verbs and adjectives.

Underline the verb that the highlighted adverb describes.

C-3PO was masterfully <u>built</u> from spare parts by Anakin Skywalker to help his mother around the home.

R2-D2 belonged to the Royal Security Forces of Naboo and served Padmé loyally.

The two droids fatefully met on Tatooine and became friends even though they were opposites.

R2-D2 boldly reacted to dangerous situations, whereas C-3PO urged caution.

Years after they first met, the pair bravely delivered a message for Princess Leia about the Death Star.

Later, R2-D2 stealthily brought Luke his lightsaber while posing as a servant.

C-3PO wisely told the story of the Galactic Civil War to the Ewoks to get them on the rebels' side.

C-3PO was blissfully unaware that he had been built by Darth Vader when the Sith was just a boy.

Galactic Glossary

A **glossary** is an alphabetical list of words and their definitions. Use the glossary to answer the questions.

word

part of speech

droid (droyd)
(noun) a robot
Anakin built the *droid* by using spare parts.

pronunciation

definition

how it is used in a sentence

---

dark side (dark'-sid)
(noun): the evil aspect of the Force

Anakin has turned to the *dark side*.

Force (fors)
(noun): the energy created by all living things

The *Force* is what gives a Jedi his or her power.

Force-sensitive (fors sen-se-tiv)
(adjective): strong awareness of the Force and the ability to connect to it

Qui-Gon Jinn first noticed that Anakin was *Force-sensitive*.

Jedi (je'-di)
(noun): members of an order who use the Force to promote peace and justice

The *Jedi* were the guardians of peace in the Old Republic.

lightsaber (lit sa-ber)
(noun): a sword with a blade that gets its power from a kyber crystal

Luke's first *lightsaber* was blue.

Padawan (pod'-a-won)
(noun): Jedi in training

Life as a *Padawan* may be tough, but you find out who you are.

Sith (sith)
1. (noun): member of an order who uses the Force for evil

2. (noun): an alien species with red skin and tentacles that is prone to using the dark side of the Force

We take what we want because we are powerful *Sith*.

1. What word means "a sword with a blade that gets its power from a kyber crystal"?

    _____

2. According to the definitions of **Force-sensitive** and **Jedi**, does a Jedi have a strong awareness of the Force? _____

3. How many syllables are in **Jedi**? _____

4. What part of speech is **Padawan**? _____

5. How many definitions are there for **Sith**? _____

6. If **planet** were added to this glossary, between what two words would it go? _____

7. Write a sentence using **droid**.

    _____

    _____

8. Write a sentence using another word from the glossary.

    _____

    _____

Pilot Parts of Speech

Imagine that you have discovered a new Imperial Pilot Academy. Fill in the blanks.

PILOT STUDENT RULES

Welcome to Imperial Pilot Academy! Here you will learn to be _____. But you must
<u>(adjective)</u>
follow the rules.

1. Imperial pilots keep their rooms _____. You must _____
   <u>(adjective)</u>   <u>(verb)</u>
   your room every day.

2. Arrive at breakfast by 7 a.m. After all, you wouldn't want to miss our
   delicious _____.
   <u>(plural noun)</u>

3. No _____ fights in the cafeteria!
   <u>(noun)</u>

4. Attend all classes and listen to your teachers. They are _____.
   <u>(adjective)</u>

5. Absolutely no _____ in the classroom!
   <u>(plural noun)</u>

6. Plan to study _____.
   <u>(adjective)</u>

7. Lights out by 9 p.m. Remember: Early to bed, early to rise, makes pilots
   _____, _____, and _____.
   <u>(adjective)</u>   <u>(adjective)</u>   <u>(adjective)</u>

I sincerely hope you _____ a lot while at Imperial Pilot Academy.
<u>(verb)</u>

Combining Forces

A **conjunction** is a word used to combine clauses or sentences.

Read each sentence. Then fill in the blank with the correct conjunction to combine the sentences.

Mace Windu was a Jedi. He was a member of the High Council.
Mace Windu was a Jedi __and__ a member of the High Council.

`and` `but`

He realized the Sith had returned. He learned about Darth Maul.
He realized the Sith had returned _____ he learned about Darth Maul.

`since` `when`

Windu thought Anakin Skywalker was too old for Jedi training.
   Qui-Gon Jinn decided to train Anakin anyway.
Windu thought Anakin Skywalker was too old for Jedi training, _____
   Qui-Gon Jinn decided to train Anakin anyway.

`when` `but`

Windu went to Geonosis. He learned that Obi-Wan was there with Padmé
   and Anakin.
Windu went to Geonosis _____ he learned that Obi-Wan was there
   with Padmé and Anakin.

`but` `since`

Windu fought in the Battle of Geonosis. He defeated Jango Fett.
Windu fought in the Battle of Geonosis, _____ he defeated Jango Fett.

`where` `but`

Windu would have won the lightsaber duel with Chancellor Palpatine.
   Anakin joined in and cut off Windu's hand.
Windu would have won the lightsaber duel with Chancellor Palpatine,
   _____ Anakin joined in and cut off Windu's hand.

`but` `while`

After the Battle of Endor

A **simple sentence** has one **independent clause**, which is a clause that can stand alone as a complete sentence.

> Luke used the Force.

A **compound sentence** has two independent clauses joined by a comma and a conjunction.

> The Ewoks live on Endor, and they build houses in treetops.
> ↑   ↑   ↑
> **independent clause**   **comma and conjunction**   **independent clause**

Underline each simple sentence. Circle the comma and conjunction in each compound sentence.

The Empire needed a shield for the second Death Star. Imperial troops selected the forest moon of Endor, and they built a shield generator to protect the Death Star. The rebels wanted to disable the shield generator. They planned a surprise attack, and the Ewoks joined their side. An Ewok distracted the stormtroopers, and the rebels entered the Empire outpost. The rebels fought bravely, but they were caught. The Ewoks attacked stormtroopers with bows, arrows, traps, and slingshots. This helped the rebels defeat the Imperial troops, and it helped them destroy the shield generator. The rebels and Ewoks won the Battle of Endor together.

It All Depends

A **complex sentence** has an independent clause and at least one **dependent clause**. A dependent clause is a clause that cannot stand alone as a complete sentence.

> When Anakin was a young boy, he wanted to train as a Jedi.
> ↑ dependent clause   ↑ independent clause

The words in the box below often begin a **dependent clause**. Read the words, and circle the **dependent clause** in each **complex sentence**.

> after   because   which   while   when   once

Because he sensed anger in Anakin, Yoda didn't want the boy trained as a Jedi.

Obi-Wan insisted on training the boy, which was Qui-Gon Jinn's dying wish.

Once Anakin became Darth Vader, there was no going back.

Because Padmé loved Anakin, she was upset that he turned to the dark side.

After Anakin fell into the lava lake, he was rebuilt as Darth Vader.

Luke and Leia didn't know about each other because their identities were kept secret.

Leia grew up in a palace, while Luke lived a simpler life on a moisture farm.

When Luke told Leia she was his sister, she was happy.

Han was also happy because it meant that he could express his feelings of love for Leia.

Rebels Without a Clause

Write whether each sentence is simple, compound, or complex.

Luke worked on the moisture farm with his Uncle Owen, and he always wondered what had happened to his real father.

_____

When Luke was cleaning R2-D2, the droid played an urgent holographic message from Princess Leia to Obi-Wan Kenobi.

_____

"I wonder if he means Old Ben Kenobi," said Luke as he remembered the old hermit with a similar name.

_____

When Uncle Owen mentioned that Obi-Wan Kenobi knew Luke's father, Luke became even more curious.

_____

R2-D2 escaped to deliver the message to Obi-Wan Kenobi, and Luke and C-3PO found him in the desert.

_____

They were ambushed by a group of Tusken Raiders.

_____

Obi-Wan saved them by making a sound that scared off the Tusken Raiders.

_____

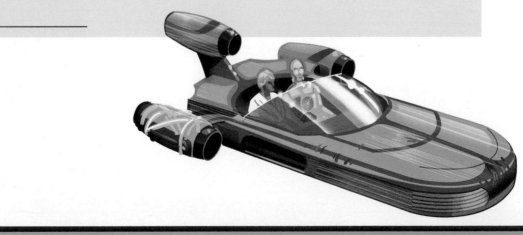

Rebellion Readiness

Fill out the survey.

REBEL ALLIANCE READINESS

Thank you for your interest in joining the Rebel Alliance.
Please fill out this survey to test your readiness.
May the Force be with you!

Full Name

Home Planet

_____

Languages Spoken

Age

_____

Rebel Alliance Skills (piloting, strategy, leadership, etc.)

_____

Personal Traits (bravery, compassion, loyalty, wisdom, etc.)

_____

Are any of your family members a part of the Rebel Alliance?
Yes   No   I don't know.

On a scale of 1 to 10, how good are you with droids (10 being the best)?
1   2   3   4   5   6   7   8   9   10

Why would you make a good rebel? Support your point of view with reasons.

_____

_____

_____

_____

Yoda Origami

Follow the **directions** to make an origami Yoda. Then answer the questions.

Supplies:

A piece of notebook or printer paper
A pencil

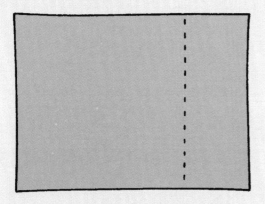

1. Lay the paper widthwise.

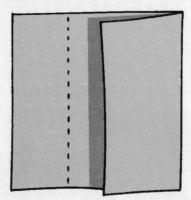

2. Fold one side over so that it reaches a little more than halfway across the paper.

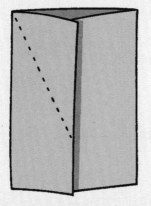

3. Then fold the other side a little over that.

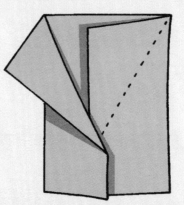

4. Fold one side at a diagonal.

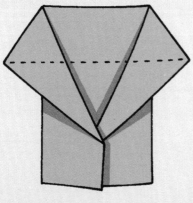

5. Fold the other side at a diagonal.

6. Fold the top over. Draw a face on Yoda.

What supplies do you need to complete this project?

_____

What is the first step?

_____

What step comes after folding both sides at a diagonal?

_____

Based on the picture that goes with the direction, what does
widthwise mean?

    a. longer from top to bottom

    b. longer from side to side

Why did you need the pencil?

_____

How did the pictures help you to follow
the instructions?

_____

_____

_____

_____

Map of the Galaxy

Examine the map of the galaxy. (Note that it includes only some of the planets.) Then answer the questions with complete sentences.

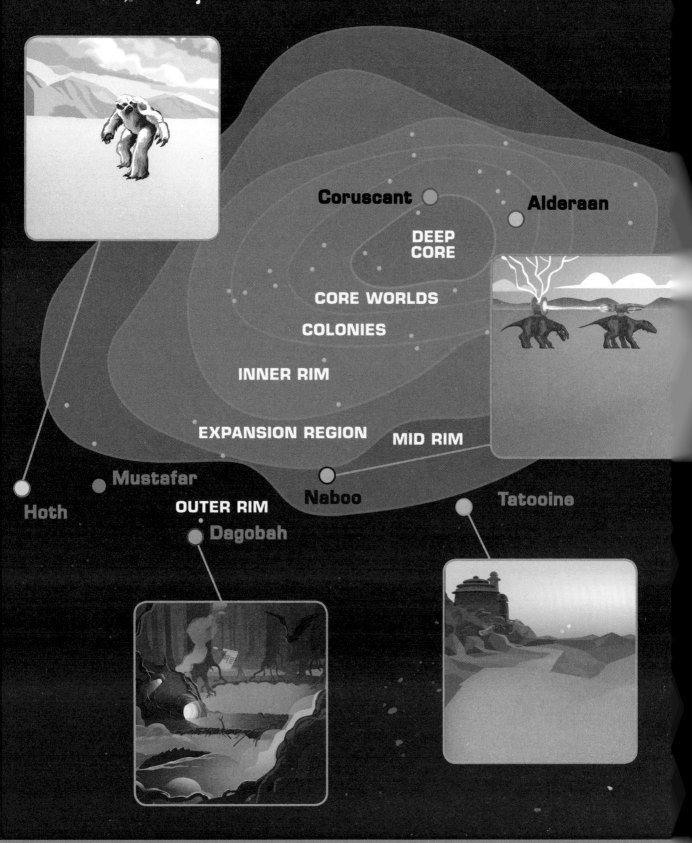

Coruscant

Alderaan

DEEP CORE

CORE WORLDS

COLONIES

INNER RIM

EXPANSION REGION

MID RIM

Mustafar

Naboo

Tatooine

Hoth

OUTER RIM

Dagobah

Is Padmé's home planet, Naboo, a Mid Rim or an Outer Rim planet?

_____

Based on the map, is the climate on Hoth hot or cold?

_____

Luke worked on a moisture farm on a desert planet. Which planet was it?

_____

Which is closer to the capital planet of Coruscant: Leia's planet, Alderaan, or Luke's planet, Tatooine?

_____

Luke was trained on a swamp planet. Which planet was it?

_____

Based on the pictures, on which planet would you most want to live and why? Support your point of view with reasons.

_____

_____

_____

_____

My Favorite Lightsaber

Imagine that your friends voted on which color lightsaber they like best.

7 said green

3 said blue

4 said purple

1 said red

(Uh-oh. Better keep your eye on that one!)

Make a **pictograph** showing the votes by drawing one lightsaber for each vote.

Favorite Lightsaber

Blue   Green   Purple   Red

A **conclusion** is a summary or judgment drawn from the information given.

Write conclusions that you can make based on this pictograph.

1. The red lightsaber is least popular.

2.

3.

Lando Takes the Lead

Temporal words help show the order in which events happen.
Lando Calrissian is figuring out how to rescue Han Solo from Jabba's palace. Imagine that you are helping him write a plan. Fill in the correct temporal words from the boxes.

first   next   then   finally

_____, I will go to the palace disguised as a guard. I'll be there to help fight in case anything goes wrong. _____, we will send R2-D2 and C-3PO as gifts to Jabba the Hutt. In return, we will ask him to give us Han Solo. If that doesn't work, Leia will go to Jabba disguised as a bounty hunter who has captured Chewie. She will secretly free Han. She will _____ escape with Han, Chewie, and me. _____, if all else fails, Luke will make his way into the palace using Jedi mind tricks and ask Jabba to return Han. Surely one of these tactics will work. Ready. On three. One, two, three, go team!

The Coruscant Star

Read the breaking news.

Rebels Wanted After Death Star Escape

Four enemies of the Galactic Empire are on the run after escaping the Empire's moon-sized space station, the Death Star. They are Princess Leia Organa of the former planet Alderaan, Luke Skywalker, Han Solo, and a Wookiee known as Chewbacca. A fifth rebel, Obi-Wan Kenobi, died during the escape. The rebels also have two droids with them, an R2 unit and a protocol droid.

Princess Leia was being held captive on the Death Star. She had stolen the space station's confidential plans and loaded them onto an R2 unit. As punishment, Grand Moff Tarkin ordered her homeland of Alderaan to be destroyed. The move shows just how powerful the Death Star is—and how important it is that the rebels not learn its secrets.

Unfortunately, the Death Star plans fell into the rebel hands of Skywalker, Solo, Kenobi, and Chewbacca. Their ship, the *Millennium Falcon*, was pulled onto the Death Star by its tractor beam. Once there, Skywalker and Solo disguised themselves as stormtroopers and set Organa free.

Skywalker, Organa, Solo, and Chewbacca made their way to the *Millennium Falcon*. There, they found Kenobi battling the brave Lord Vader. Vader defeated Kenobi. But in the confusion, the rebels escaped on the *Millennium Falcon*. Starfighters chased the rebel ship but did not catch it. The escapees are thought to be bringing the Death Star plans to the rebel troops.

If any of these outlaws are seen, Imperial authorities should be contacted immediately.

Chronological order means the order in which things happened in time, first to last.

Put the events in chronological order by numbering them from 1 to 4.

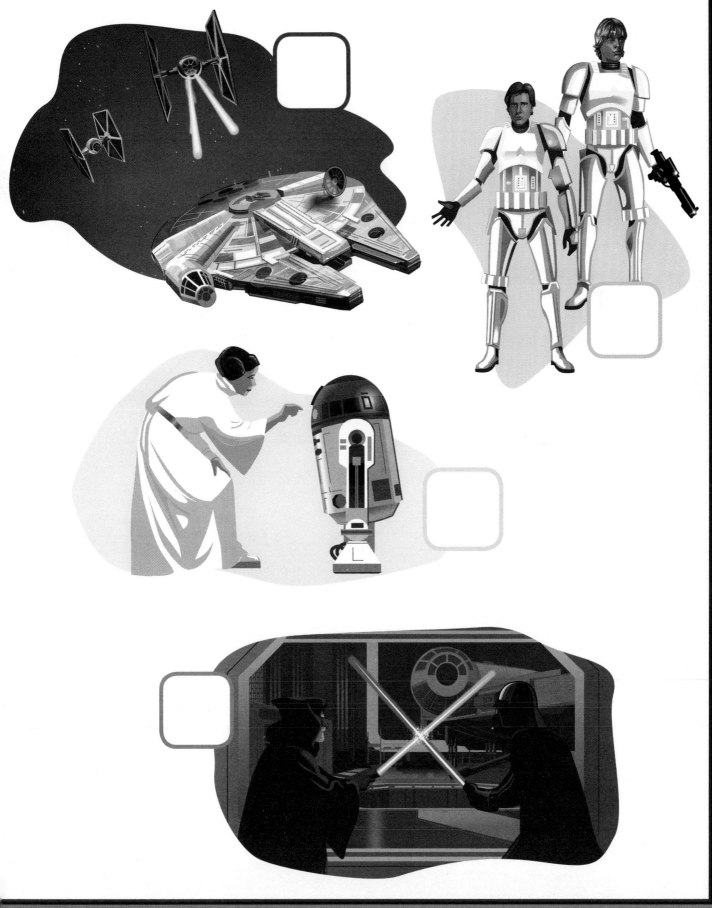

A Hairy Situation

Linking words and phrases show the relationship between two ideas. Words like **because**, **therefore**, and **so** show how one idea leads to another. Words like **however** and **but** show how one idea is different from another.

Below is a coded message that someone sent to the Mos Eisley Cantina. Fill in the blanks with the correct linking words and phrases from the boxes.

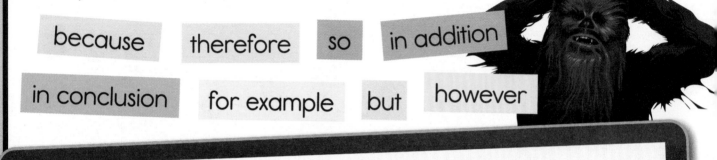

because   therefore   so   in addition

in conclusion   for example   but   however

To: Mos Eisley Cantina
From: A concerned customer

Hello,

My friend and I were really looking forward to dinner at your cantina, _____ boy, were we disappointed. We'd heard the Hungry Hutt sandwich was the best in the galaxy. _____, my friend found a bantha hair in his! He was hungry, _____ he ate the sandwich anyway. But _____ of the disgusting hair, I did not eat mine. _____, we would like our money back. _____, I plan to tell the other smugglers about the hair as soon as possible. You really should have checked our food before giving it to us. Making a Wookiee angry is a bad idea. _____, when a droid didn't let my friend win at holochess, he pulled his antennae off. _____, we will never again eat at your cantina unless we are really, really hungry.

Worst Wishes,
A concerned customer

Write a polite reply to the customer's letter. Use at least four of the linking words and phrases from the boxes.

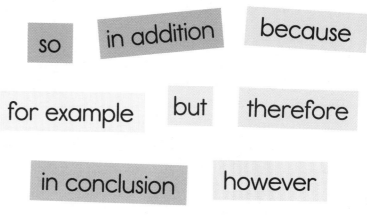

so   in addition   because

for example   but   therefore

in conclusion   however

To: Concerned customer
From: Mos Eisley Cantina

_____

_____

_____

_____

_____

_____

_____

_____

Comparing Characters

Read the Jedi trading cards.

ANAKIN SKYWALKER
HOMEWORLD: Tatooine
SPECIES: Human
MENTOR: Obi-Wan Kenobi
LIGHTSABER COLOR: blue

A slave on Tatooine, Anakin's Force-sensitivity was discovered at age nine. At first, the Jedi Council thought he was too old to become a Jedi. But they finally agreed to allow Obi-Wan to train Anakin. Anakin became a great Jedi, known in the Clone Wars as "the Hero with No Fear." But when Anakin discovered that his mother had been attacked on Tatooine, his anger overcame him. He turned to the dark side.

LUKE SKYWALKER
HOMEWORLD: Tatooine
SPECIES: Human
MENTOR: Obi-Wan Kenobi
LIGHTSABER COLOR: first blue, then green

Born the son of Senator Padmé Amidala and Anakin Skywalker, Luke's identity was hidden for his own safety. His father, Anakin, had turned to the dark side and become Darth Vader. His Force-sensitivity was discovered when he was reunited with Obi-Wan Kenobi at age nineteen. Obi-Wan began training him to become a Jedi. Luke was an adventure seeker with strong natural piloting skills.

Comparing is describing how two or more things are alike.
Contrasting is describing how they are different.

Fill in the **Venn diagram** to show ways that Anakin and Luke are alike or different.

Anakin	Anakin and Luke	Luke
Discovered at age nine	Both Force-sensitive	Discovered at age nineteen
_____	_____	_____
_____	_____	_____
_____	_____	_____
_____	_____	_____

Use your Venn diagram to write a paragraph that compares and contrasts Anakin and Luke. Include one linking word from the boxes below in each sentence.

also   another   and   more   but

_____

_____

_____

_____

A New Leader

The evil Empire has fallen. Imagine that you could suggest a leader for the galaxy's New Republic. Read about each rebel candidate.

C-3PO served Senator Padmé Amidala for several years. Later, he joined the Rebel Alliance as R2-D2's trusted friend. C-3PO can speak seven million languages.

While serving as Senator of Alderaan, **Princess Leia** secretly helped form the Rebel Alliance with her father, Bail Organa. Under her leadership, the rebels overthrew the Empire.

R2-D2 played many roles in overthrowing the Empire. He delivered the Death Star plans to the rebels, helped them to escape the Death Star, and saved Luke Skywalker from the Sarlacc.

As a military leader during the Clone Wars, **Chewbacca** saved Yoda from Order 66. After a brief career as a smuggler, he joined the Rebel Alliance as a soldier.

During the Galactic Civil War, **Luke Skywalker** trained as a Jedi. Using the Force, he destroyed the Death Star and Emperor Palpatine.

Lando Calrissian was the mayor of Cloud City, a town famous throughout the galaxy for its luxurious lifestyle. He joined the Rebel Alliance and helped overthrow the Empire.

Han Solo may have started out in the Galactic Civil War as a smuggler, but he soon became one of the most important rebel soldiers, saving Luke Skywalker during the Battle of Yavin.

Your Vote

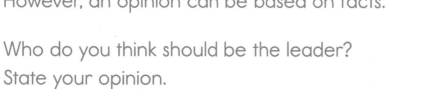

An **opinion** is a belief and not a fact.
However, an opinion can be based on facts.

Who do you think should be the leader?
State your opinion.

_____ should be the leader of the
New Republic.

List three reasons why your chosen candidate should be the new
leader. Include facts provided or facts that you know from other
sources to **support your opinion**.

_____

_____

_____

_____

_____

_____

_____

_____

_____

_____

Your Opinion

Using your notes from page 48, write a paragraph about who should be the leader and why. Begin by stating your opinion. Then give three reasons to support your opinion. Finally, end with a **conclusion** that sums up why the candidate is a good choice. Draw a picture of your candidate to go with the paragraph.

What a World!

Read about the planets.

NABOO

Naboo is a planet rich in water. Built on the Solleu River, the entire capital city of Theed has a view of the water. The city's classical architecture, vibrant colors, and peaceful atmosphere add to its beauty. At the Royal Palace, the river cascades down a cliff, forming beautiful waterfalls. Away from the city, lakes dot the countryside. Even the core of Naboo is filled with water. This is where the Gungans live. In the city of Otoh Gunga, the buildings are floating bubbles filled with breathable air. The Gungans can swim through the walls without letting water in. Most Gungans avoid the deepest core waters, which are filled with giant sea monsters. Whether they are treacherous or peaceful, Naboo's waterways are never forgotten by those who see them.

DAGOBAH

This swamp planet may be hot, foggy, and stormy, but it is not all bad. In fact, Dagobah is where Yoda lives, and it is filled with the Force. Here, Yoda was led by a swarm of fireflies to a special cave in which he hid from the Empire. In the so-called Cave of Evil, visitors can see visions of dark futures. Luke saw himself strike Darth Vader down. On this planet, Luke gained strength by racing through the thick swamps and swinging from tree to tree. He also learned the power of the Force from Yoda here.

TATOOINE

Unlike Naboo, Tatooine has almost no water at all. The planet consists of sand dunes, mesas, and canyons. Twin suns keep the planet hot year-round. In spite of the harsh conditions, the desert planet is far from deserted. Creatures include shaggy banthas, scaly dewbacks, and gigantic rontos. The Hutts rule the planet from their palaces, making their money by stealing and smuggling. In the major city of Mos Espa, the Hutts host podraces in the Mos Espa Grand Arena. They make money on the races by taking bets. Others make a living more honestly. Moisture farmers use machines to gather what little water exists on the planet. Then they sell the precious water.

ENDOR

The forest moon of Endor orbits a giant gas planet. The pine and redwood forests on this moon are teeming with life. Birdsong fills the air, and many species make their homes here. Ewoks have built glowing villages in the trees, hollowing out the trunks for their huts. Wooden furniture, furry blankets, and cooking fires create a homey environment. The huts are connected by ladders and bridges, which are lit by torches. In addition to forests, Endor has deserts, plains, oceans, and lakes. Though only a moon, Endor has an important role in history. It's where the rebels won the war against the Empire.

Dream Vacation

Pretend one of the locations above is your home. Using information provided on pages 50–51, make a travel brochure encouraging people to visit your world.

For the cover, draw a picture of your home. Then write a sentence that invites people to visit this wonderful place.

Write the inside of the brochure. Start with a sentence telling people why they should visit your world. Then write three sentences about things they can see and do. Conclude by summing up what is wonderful about this location.

_____   _____

_____   _____

_____   _____

_____   _____

_____   _____

_____   _____

_____   _____

_____   _____

_____   _____

_____   _____

Compare and Contrast

Two **sources** can describe an event differently. Read the paragraphs from two different communications about how Leia became a rebel leader.

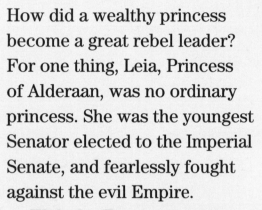

REBEL PRINCESS

How did a wealthy princess become a great rebel leader? For one thing, Leia, Princess of Alderaan, was no ordinary princess. She was the youngest Senator elected to the Imperial Senate, and fearlessly fought against the evil Empire.

With the Force strong in Leia, she was destined to bring order to the galaxy. Leia also inherited her birth mother Padmé's leadership abilities. As Senator, she criticized the Emperor's unjust rule. Meanwhile, she visited other planets to help people hurt by the Empire. Her courage and dedication helped lead to the Death Star's destruction, a turning point in the revolution. As a leader of the Rebellion, victory would be hers.

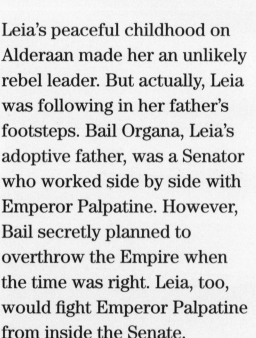

LEIA: PRINCESS, SENATOR, SPY

Leia's peaceful childhood on Alderaan made her an unlikely rebel leader. But actually, Leia was following in her father's footsteps. Bail Organa, Leia's adoptive father, was a Senator who worked side by side with Emperor Palpatine. However, Bail secretly planned to overthrow the Empire when the time was right. Leia, too, would fight Emperor Palpatine from inside the Senate.

At the early age of eighteen, she was elected Senator of Alderaan and accomplished a lot in her youth. As Senator, she criticized the Emperor for his unjust rule. Meanwhile, she helped build the Rebel Alliance with her father. After the tragic destruction of Alderaan and death of her father, Leia became an important leader of the Rebellion.

Place an **x** in each appropriate box.

WHICH ARTICLE CONTAINED THIS FACT?	"REBEL PRINCESS"	"LEIA: PRINCESS, SENATOR, SPY"
Senator Bail Organa was Leia's adoptive father.		
Padmé was Leia's mother.		
Leia became Senator at age eighteen.		
Leia inherited Padmé's leadership skills.		
Leia criticized the Emperor.		
Alderaan was destroyed.		
Leia visited other planets to help people.		
Leia was a leader of the Rebellion.		

Both sources state that Leia became Senator, but they suggest that different people influenced her ability to be a strong leader. What does the first article say? What does the second article say?

_____

_____

_____

_____

Rebel Report

An **outline** is a written plan for a report. It shows the information that will appear in the report and the order that it will be included. An outline is usually organized by letters and numbers.

Using information from the stories on page 54, fill in the outline for a report on Princess Leia. Write short phrases summarizing a supporting detail in your own words. Then write RP if it came from "Rebel Princess" or LPSS if it came from "Leia: Princess, Senator, Spy."

A. Leia accomplished a lot as a young adult.

1._____(   )

2._____(   )

B. As she grew up, it was clear that Leia had inherited abilities from her birth mother, as well as her adoptive father.

1._____(   )

2._____(   )

3._____(   )

C. Eventually, Leia became a Senator and a heroic leader of the Rebellion against the Empire.

1._____(   )

2._____(   )

A **first draft** is the first written version of the report. It can be changed and improved later. Use your outline to write a first draft of your report about Princess Leia.

Write a draft title for your report.

_____

Write a draft introduction for your report.

_____

_____

_____

Write a draft body of your report.

_____

_____

_____

_____

_____

Write a draft conclusion for your report.

_____

_____

_____

Rebel Report Continued

Just like Boba Fett on the hunt for bounty, you are on the hunt for errors. Use the checklist and the proofreading marks below to edit any mistakes in your report on page 57.

∧ **Add text**	⊙ **Add a period**	**Add missing punctuation or words**
≡ **Capitalize letter**	℘ **Take out**	◯ **Spelling error**

Grammar Checklist

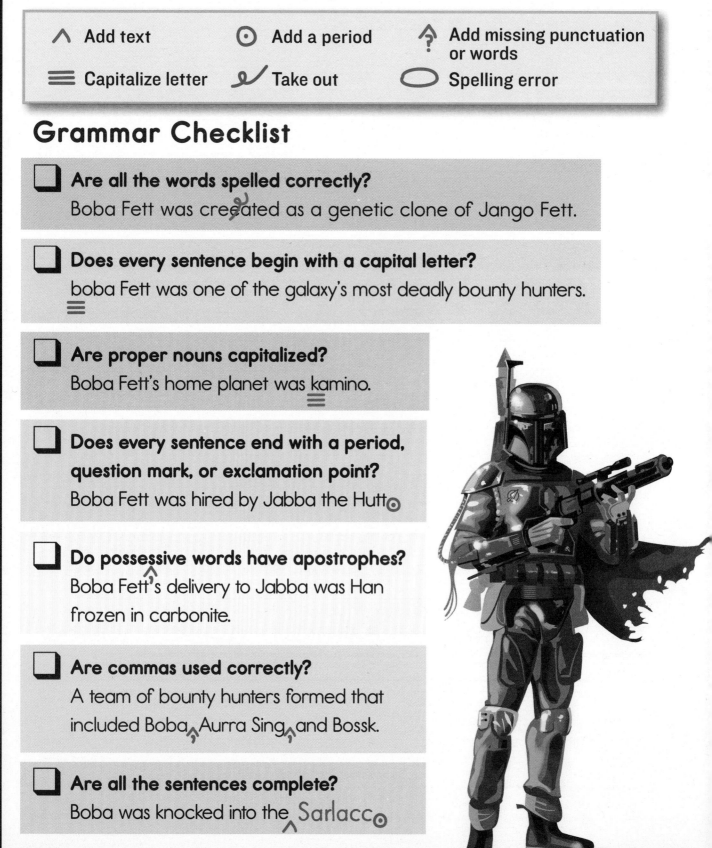

☐ **Are all the words spelled correctly?**
Boba Fett was creｅated as a genetic clone of Jango Fett.

☐ **Does every sentence begin with a capital letter?**
boba Fett was one of the galaxy's most deadly bounty hunters.

☐ **Are proper nouns capitalized?**
Boba Fett's home planet was kamino.

☐ **Does every sentence end with a period, question mark, or exclamation point?**
Boba Fett was hired by Jabba the Hutt⊙

☐ **Do possessive words have apostrophes?**
Boba Fett's delivery to Jabba was Han frozen in carbonite.

☐ **Are commas used correctly?**
A team of bounty hunters formed that included Boba, Aurra Sing, and Bossk.

☐ **Are all the sentences complete?**
Boba was knocked into the Sarlacc⊙

Rewrite your report with all your corrections.
Draw an illustration to help show the information.

_____

_____

_____

_____

_____

_____

_____

_____

_____

_____

Pretend you are giving a speech on Princess Leia.
Read your finished report aloud.

Setting the Scene

A **setting** is a place where a story happens. It also sets the **mood**, or feeling, of the story.

Create a setting by completing each activity. First, choose a planet:

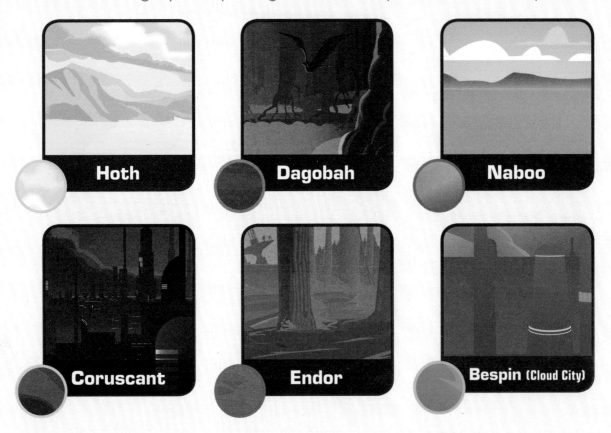

Then choose a location:

city   canyon   forest   sky   stream   swamp   snowy mountain

Next, circle a mood:

spooky   peaceful   dreary   cozy   exciting

Now write three sentences describing your setting and its mood.
Remember to use adjectives and descriptive language.

_____

_____

_____

Planet Paragraph

Using your sentences on the previous page, write a
paragraph that expands the description of your setting.
Include an introductory and concluding sentence.
Draw a picture to help show the information.

Anakin at the Start

Read the chapter.

CHAPTER ONE: YOUNG ANAKIN

Young Anakin Skywalker lived a difficult life. Both Anakin and his mother were slaves who lived on the Outer Rim planet of Tatooine. He grew up without a father in a very arid and sandy desert.

During this time, Anakin lived in Mos Espa. This spaceport city was controlled by the Hutts. Anakin worked in the scrapyard with his grouchy slave master, Watto. They sold scrap and replacement parts for starships, droids, and more. One of Anakin's jobs was to repair the salvage that came into the shop for his master. Watto controlled everything that Anakin did as his slave.

Young Anakin had many skills—he could see the future, he was a talented pilot, and he was a handy mechanic. He even built his own protocol droid, C-3PO. Though he was young, he also secretly built a podracer.

Anakin's life changed in a big way one day when Jedi Master Qui-Gon Jinn made an emergency landing on Tatooine. There he met Anakin in the scrapyard. Qui-Gon could sense the Force in young Anakin. He made a bet with Watto and won Anakin's freedom from slavery. Anakin became a free person and left Tatooine to travel with Qui-Gon and his apprentice, Obi-Wan Kenobi.

A **main idea** tells what the story is about. **Details** are descriptions and events that support the main idea.

Answer the questions.

What is the main idea of this chapter?
- **a.** Anakin grew up in the desert.
- **b.** Anakin had a hard life as a child.
- **c.** Watto is a bad character.

Write the sentence in this chapter that states the main idea.

_____

What does _arid_ mean in the first paragraph?
- **a.** rainy
- **b.** grassy
- **c.** dry

What detail from the story shows what Anakin's days were like as a slave?
- **a.** He grew up without a father.
- **b.** He repaired the salvage that came into the scrapyard.
- **c.** He was young.

Write three details that show Anakin's abilities.

_____

_____

_____

What detail explains how Anakin learned to be skilled at fixing and building things?

_____

_____

CHAPTER TWO: ANAKIN THE PADAWAN

Jedi Master Qui-Gon Jinn believed that Anakin was the Chosen One. He believed that the boy would restore order and balance to the galaxy. Qui-Gon and his apprentice, Obi-Wan, brought young Anakin to Coruscant. There, Anakin was presented to the Jedi High Council. Qui-Gon could sense the Force in Anakin and wanted to train him as a Jedi. The Jedi High Council refused. They found fear in Anakin and would not let him be trained as a Jedi. Qui-Gon still believed.

Young Anakin traveled with Qui-Gon and Obi-Wan to the planet of Naboo on a mission. They were to protect Queen Amidala. While there, a battle broke out and Anakin hid in the cockpit of a starfighter. He accidentally started the autopilot and launched into space. While flying, he was hit by a vulture droid. His damaged starfighter unexpectedly flew into the hangar of an enemy command ship. He fired some torpedoes and ended up destroying the enemy ship! This brought an end to the battle on Naboo. Anakin had helped win the fight.

Jedi Master Qui-Gon was killed in a lightsaber battle against the enemy, Darth Maul. Before he died, he asked Obi-Wan to train and care for young Anakin. He still believed that Anakin was the Chosen One and needed to be trained. Obi-Wan convinced the Jedi High Council, and Anakin became his Padawan. Anakin's Jedi training had begun.

Draw a star next to the correct answer.

Which sentence tells the main idea of this text?

☐ They found fear in Anakin and would not let him be trained as a Jedi.

☐ Jedi Master Qui-Gon Jinn believed that Anakin was the Chosen One.

Which idea in the story is NOT related to the main idea?

☐ Before he died, he asked Obi-Wan to train and care for young Anakin.

☐ Jedi Master Qui-Gon was killed in a lightsaber battle against the enemy.

What detail explains how Anakin begins his training?

☐ Obi-Wan convinced the Jedi High Council, and Anakin became his Padawan.

☐ He fired some torpedoes and ended up destroying the enemy ship!

Based on details in the story, why didn't the High Council want to train Anakin?

☐ They found fear in Anakin.

☐ Darth Vader was an evil commander.

Droid Drama

Read this retelling of events
from C-3PO's life.

Of C-3PO's many sufferings, his journey to Tatooine was the worst. It started when stormtroopers invaded his starship. He was doomed!

Next R2-D2 disappeared, and C-3PO was forced to search for his friend while under enemy fire. He found him hiding in an escape pod. R2-D2 wanted C-3PO to exit the starship with him. Hurtling through space in a metal ball—C-3PO thought that was a horrible idea! But that's exactly what R2-D2 planned to do. So, C-3PO unwisely decided to go along with him. They were friends, after all.

They landed in the middle of the desert. C-3PO had never seen such a desolate place. R2-D2 suggested they head toward the mountains. C-3PO thought that was a terrible idea—such a difficult walk could cause their limbs to freeze up. The friends quarreled and headed in separate directions.

C-3PO didn't know it at the time, but R2-D2 had been captured by Jawas, who planned to resell him. Luckily, C-3PO and R2-D2 met up on the Jawa's sandcrawler. Though R2-D2 is stubborn, C-3PO was happy to see him. Soon C-3PO was purchased by a moisture farmer and his nephew, Luke. He convinced them to buy R2-D2, too. He didn't want to leave his friend behind on such an unfriendly planet.

Troublemaker that he is, R2-D2 disappeared in the night. Luke and C-3PO went to find him the next day and got attacked by Sand People. C-3PO's arm was torn off. He felt once again that he was born to suffer. And it seemed like R2-D2's fault!

Fortunately, they were taken in by a kind man named Ben Kenobi. C-3PO had been through a lot, and so he powered down for a well-deserved nap.

A **character** is a person, or something that behaves like a person, in a story.

Answer the questions.

Who are the two main characters in the story?

_____

Which statement describes how C-3PO feels about R2-D2?
 a. C-3PO wants to be just like R2-D2.
 b. C-3PO thinks R2-D2 is a troublemaker.
 c. C-3PO doesn't worry about R2-D2 because he can take care of himself.

What event in the story shows that C-3PO cares about R2-D2?
 a. C-3PO parts ways with R2-D2 after the two argue in the desert.
 b. C-3PO convinces Luke and his uncle to buy R2-D2, too.
 c. C-3PO powers down for a nap.

How does C-3PO feel about his time on Tatooine?
 a. Proud. He is a hero!
 b. Excited. Adventure is fun!
 c. Frustrated. He detests danger.

Support your answer to the above question by finding a line from the story that describes how C-3PO feels. Write it here.

_____

_____

Which adjective best describes R2-D2?
 a. bold
 b. timid
 c. brilliant
 d. charming

Yoda and the Skywalkers

Read the stories.

YODA and ANAKIN

Yoda first met Anakin Skywalker during a Jedi Council meeting. Young Anakin had been brought from his remote home planet of Tatooine to the big city planet of Coruscant. Here, Jedi Master Qui-Gon Jinn asked the council for permission to train the boy. Yoda, a revered council member, wondered if Anakin was a bad fit for Jedi training. For one thing, the boy was too old. He should have been raised as a Jedi from the time he was a toddler. Second, Yoda thought Anakin's memories of his mother would cloud his judgment. Qui-Gon's request was denied. But when Qui-Gon was killed by a mysterious Sith, Obi-Wan Kenobi insisted on training Anakin. After all, Qui-Gon had thought that Anakin was the Chosen One. Yoda reluctantly agreed.

But Yoda's misgivings came true when Anakin turned to the dark side. Anakin became Darth Vader, apprentice to Darth Sidious. And it was Sidious who gave Order 66, demanding that all Jedi be killed.

YODA and LUKE

After Order 66, Obi-Wan Kenobi and Yoda went into hiding. Obi-Wan died, so only his spirit remained. But Yoda was still alive on the remote swamp planet of Dagobah. A Force-sensitive young man named Luke traveled to the planet to find Yoda. Yoda pretended to be someone else but offered to lead Luke to Yoda. In this way, he hoped to see whether Luke had Jedi potential. When Luke became impatient with the disguised Master, Yoda doubted the young Skywalker. Yoda thought Luke was too much like Anakin—impatient, angry, and too old for Jedi training. Yoda knew all too well the dangers of training such a knight. But the spirit of Obi-Wan convinced Yoda to give Luke a chance. Yoda trained Luke in the dangerous swamp, telling him, "Try not. Do or do not. There is no try." Unlike his father, Anakin, Luke stayed true to the Jedi path and helped restore order to the galaxy.

Word choice refers to picking words that mean exactly what you intend to communicate.

Answer the questions about the stories from pages 68 and 69.

The story says, "Yoda, a revered council member, wondered if Anakin was a bad fit for Jedi training." The word choice "wondered if" shows that Yoda was unsure. If Yoda was *sure* that Anakin was a bad fit for Jedi training, which of the word choices below should be used instead?

    a. suspected that

    b. knew that

    c. had heard that

The story states, "Yoda thought Anakin's memories of his mother would cloud his judgment." What does *cloud* mean?

    a. confuse

    b. destroy

    c. improve

The story says, "But when Qui-Gon was killed by a mysterious Sith, Obi-Wan Kenobi insisted on training Anakin." What words mean the same thing as "insisted on training"?

    a. wondered about training

    b. asked about training

    c. demanded to train

What are Yoda's reasons for thinking Anakin shouldn't be trained to be a Jedi?

1. _____

2. _____

Pretend that you are Obi-Wan Kenobi. Write three reasons why you think Yoda should train Luke, even though you were wrong about his father. Choose words that will convince the reader.

1. _____

2. _____

3. _____

The Empire Strikes Back

Read the following scenes.

In the swamp on Dagobah, Luke sees a vision of Leia and Han in trouble. He loads his X-wing and prepares to leave Yoda. Yoda calls to him, "Luke! You must complete the training."

Luke replies, "I can't keep the vision out of my head. They're my friends. I've got to help them."

"You must not go!" Yoda implores.

Luke replies, "But Han and Leia will die if I don't."

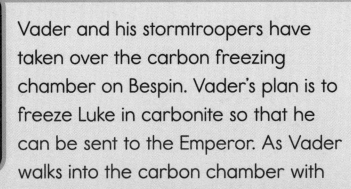

Vader and his stormtroopers have taken over the carbon freezing chamber on Bespin. Vader's plan is to freeze Luke in carbonite so that he can be sent to the Emperor. As Vader walks into the carbon chamber with his prisoners, he says, "I do not want the Emperor's prize damaged. We will test it . . . on Captain Solo."

Luke arrives on Bespin to save Han and Leia, but falls into Vader's trap. In the control room, he battles Lord Vader. Their lightsabers meet and sparks fly. Vader pushes Luke backward, saying, "You are beaten. It is useless to resist. Don't let yourself be destroyed as Obi-Wan did."

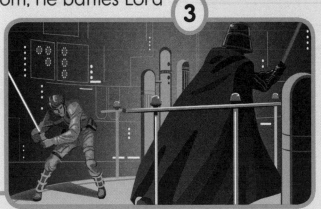

Mood is the feeling shown in an illustration or piece of writing.

Use the images and scenes on the previous page to answer the questions.

What word best describes the mood of the first image?

foreboding (suggesting that something bad will happen)

exhilaration (happiness and excitement)

humdrum (boring)

Circle all of the phrases from the first scene that reflect the mood.

Luke replies, "They're my friends."

Luke sees a vision of Leia and Han in trouble.

"You must not go!" Yoda implores.

He loads his X-wing.

What is the mood in the second scene? How does the image show this?

_____

_____

_____

Which sentence in the third scene describes the mood?

"You are beaten."

Luke arrives on Bespin.

Their lightsabers meet.

Write a paragraph to finish the story begun on page 71. First, think of the mood you want to convey. Then write the paragraph. Finally, draw a picture to go with the paragraph.

Mood:_____

_____

_____

_____

_____

Skywalker in the Lead

Read the chapter.

Podracing was a dangerous racing sport on Tatooine. Pilots raced podracers, which were small and fast. Each had a cockpit pulled by two powerful engines. Pilots completed fast and dangerous laps around a track while crowds watched and cheered for the leaders.

The Boonta Eve Classic was an important event—it was the largest podrace on Tatooine. During one annual race, young Anakin Skywalker won his freedom from slavery! Jedi Master Qui-Gon Jinn discovered Anakin and made a bet with his owner, Watto. If Anakin won the race, he would be freed. If Anakin lost the race, Watto would win Qui-Gon's starship.

Although Anakin was young, he had been building his blue and silver podracer in secret. He believed it to be the fastest ever created. He raced it against seventeen other pilots, including the fierce Sebulba. Sebulba flew a large orange podracer. He was known for his vicious racing tricks. He would often smash into his competition, fire a built-in flamethrower, or use other illegal weapons.

After a flag ceremony in the Grand Arena, the podracers' engines fired and the race began. Anakin's engines flooded and died. He was stalled. He got them restarted and zoomed out of the arena at the back of the pack. The first lap was filled with many dangers. Several podracers crashed and exploded, and Tusken Raiders shot at some of the pilots as they flew by. Anakin remained focused and determined as he finished his first lap. The crowds cheered, but C-3PO worried, "He has to complete two more circuits? Oh dear!"

Anakin's racing skills helped him gain on the pack during his second lap. Sebulba was worried about the competition. He secretly unhooked a strap on Anakin's engine. Anakin's podracer bounced and flew out of control. He remained calm and concentrated. He grabbed the strap and rehooked it to his engine.

By the third and last lap, he caught up with the leader, Sebulba. The announcer roared, "At the start of the third and final lap, Sebulba is in the lead, closely followed by Skywalker . . ."

Sebulba used one of his racing tricks and forced Anakin off the course. He flew onto a service ramp. Anakin used his pilot skills again and took the lead. "Amazing . . . a controlled thrust and he's back on course! What a move!" the announcer exclaimed.

Anakin and Sebulba raced side by side down the last leg of the race. Sebulba laughed and crashed into Anakin's podracer again and again, trying to win the race. Their podracers became stuck together. Both pilots struggled to unhook the pods and keep control. All of a sudden, Anakin's steering arm broke. Sebulba's podracer flew off of the course and exploded.

Young Anakin was safe. He crossed the finish line in first place and won the race! The announcer declared, "It's Skywalker! The crowd is going nuts!"

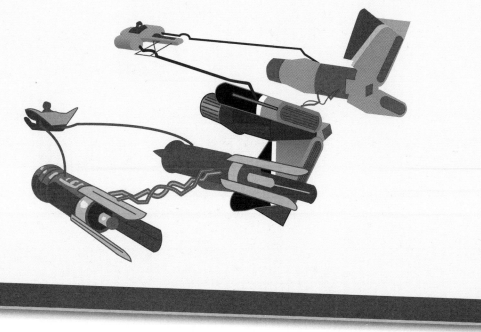

Answer the questions.

Retell what happened to Sebulba.

_____

_____

_____

What did Sebulba do to race unfairly?

_____

_____

_____

Why do you think Anakin raced fairly, even when Sebulba didn't?

_____

_____

Describe Anakin using three of the six adjectives in the boxes:

skilled   disloyal   focused   lazy   determined   selfish

_____

_____

_____

Describe a time when you played or competed fairly. Where were you? Who were you with? How did others play or compete? How did it feel?

_____

_____

_____

_____

Vile Verses

A **poem** is a piece of writing that has elements of song, such as rhythm, rhyme, careful word choice, and the expression of emotion. Poems are often divided into groups of lines called **stanzas**.

Read aloud the poem written about Kylo Ren.

It's Not Easy Being Mean

It's not easy being mean.
Would he rather be doing ordinary things?
Like training with Rey, or racing his dad
In a podrace, or something heartwarming like that?

It's not easy being mean,
Having to serve Supreme Leader Snoke,
When he really is a liar and a cheat,
And a pain in the neck as a boss as well.

But mean's the way he has to be.
It's how his fear and anger made him.
And mean has made him fight bravely,
And rule mightily, and talk huskily, and build deadly things.

When mean is all that he can be,
It can make him pine for his dad, his mom.
But maybe one day they'll also be mean,
And together they'll rule the galaxy.

Answer the questions about the poem "It's Not Easy Being Mean."

Underline all the reasons given by the author of the poem for why it's not easy being mean.
- **a.** He might prefer to be training with Rey.
- **b.** The Starkiller Base is going to be hard to rebuild.
- **c.** It makes him pine for his mom and dad.
- **d.** He might prefer to be racing his dad in a podrace.
- **e.** Snoke is a difficult boss.

Based on clues in the last stanza, what does "pine for" mean?
- **a.** hope to reunite with
- **b.** fight with a lightsaber
- **c.** speak on one's behalf

According to the author, in the third stanza, what conclusions can be drawn from the word choices "fight bravely" and "rule mightily"?
- **a.** Kylo Ren is ashamed of himself for being mean.
- **b.** In a way, Kylo Ren is proud of the mean things he does.
- **c.** Kylo Ren thinks that being mean is a cowardly decision.

What does "pain in the neck" mean in the second stanza?
- **a.** a hurting neck
- **b.** charming
- **c.** annoying

What might Han Solo and Leia say about Kylo Ren's plan to rule the galaxy together?

_____

_____

_____

Circle which statement you agree with.

It is easier to be nice than it is to be mean.

It is easier to be mean than it is to be nice.

Write two sentences that support your answer.

_____

_____

Imagine that you are Leia. Write a poem that responds to the poem about Kylo Ren.

_____

_____

_____

_____

_____

_____

_____

_____

_____

_____

_____

_____

_____

_____

_____

The Sister Scene

Read the script for a scene from *Return of the Jedi* aloud and act out the different parts.

Characters: LUKE and LEIA

Setting: the forest moon of ENDOR, in a quiet part of
the Ewok village at night

LEIA: Luke, what's wrong?

LUKE: Leia...do you remember your mother?
Your real mother?

LEIA: Just a little bit. She died when I was very young.

LUKE: What do you remember?

LEIA: Just...images, really. Feelings.

LUKE: Tell me.

LEIA: She was very beautiful. Kind, but...sad.
Why are you asking me all this?

LUKE: I have no memory of my mother. I never knew her.

LEIA: Luke, tell me. What's troubling you?

LUKE: Vader is here...now, on this moon.

LEIA: How do you know?

LUKE: I felt his presence. He's come for me. He can feel
when I'm near. That's why I have to go. As long as I
stay, I'm endangering the group and our mission
here. I have to face him.

LEIA: Why?

LUKE: He's my father.

LEIA: Your father?

LUKE: There's more. It won't be easy for you to hear it, but you must. If I don't make it back, you're the only hope for the Alliance.

(Leia moves away, as if to deny it.)

LEIA: Luke, don't talk that way. You have a power I—I don't understand and could never have.

LUKE: You're wrong, Leia. You have that power, too. In time you'll learn to use it as I have. The Force is strong in my family. My father has it… I have it…and…my sister has it.

(Leia stares into his eyes. She begins to understand.)

LUKE: Yes. It's you, Leia.

LEIA: I know. Somehow…I've always known.

LUKE: Then you know why I have to face him.

LEIA: No! Luke, run away, far away. If he can feel your presence, then leave this place. I wish I could go with you.

LUKE: No, you don't. You've always been strong.

LEIA: But why must you confront him?

LUKE: Because…there is a good in him. I've felt it. He won't turn me over to the Emperor. I can save him. I can turn him back to the good side. I have to try.

Studying the Script

Answer the questions about the scene from *Return of the Jedi* on pages 80 and 81.

What is the setting?

_____

_____

What does Leia remember about her mother?

_____

_____

Why must Luke face Vader?

_____

_____

In this scene, what is the first action described?

_____

_____

What does Leia do when she learns that she is Luke's sister?

_____

_____

A Favorite Scene

Choose two or three of the characters below and outline your favorite scene about them.

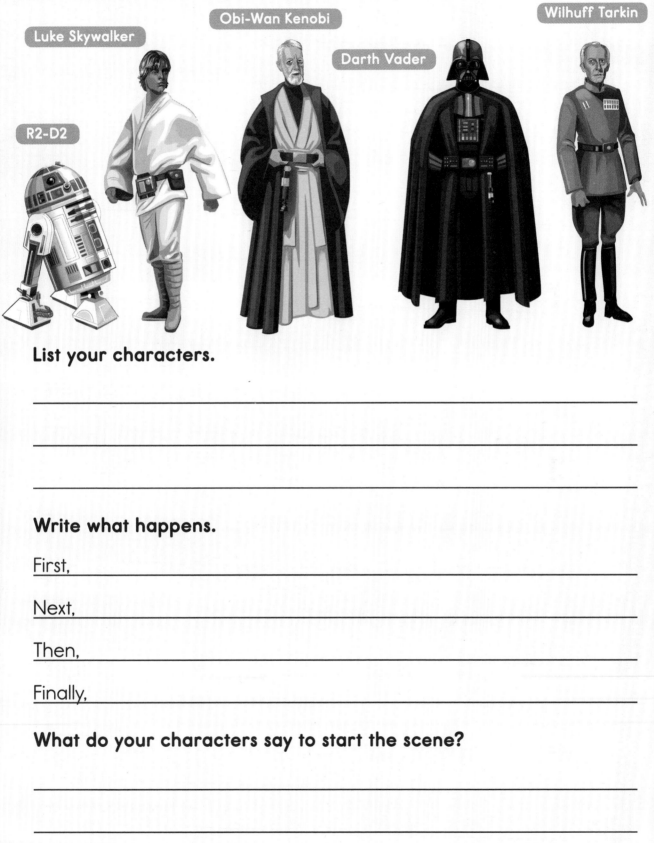

Wilhuff Tarkin

Obi-Wan Kenobi

Luke Skywalker

Darth Vader

R2-D2

List your characters.

_____

_____

_____

Write what happens.

First, _____

Next, _____

Then, _____

Finally, _____

What do your characters say to start the scene?

_____

_____

Write your favorite scene with dialogue using your outline from the previous page. Then read the scene aloud and act out the different parts.

Title: _____

Characters: _____

Setting: _____

_____

_____

_____

_____

_____

_____

_____

_____

_____

_____

_____

_____

A **set** is the scenery and furniture used onstage in a play or a movie to show the setting where the play takes place. Draw a picture of the set for your scene.

What Happens Next?

Finish the story by following the prompts.

While on the planet Coruscant, Senator Padmé Amidala is targeted in an attack. She survives, but Supreme Chancellor Sheev Palpatine suggests that she needs protection. Padmé talks with Jedi Knight Obi-Wan Kenobi and Anakin Skywalker, his apprentice. They offer to protect her, and she . . .

Describe what Padmé decides to do with Obi-Wan and Anakin's offer.

_____

_____

_____

Write a dialogue between Obi-Wan and Anakin in which they make a plan for how to keep Padmé safe.

_____

_____

_____

_____

Describe a mission the two try to accomplish.

_____

_____

_____

Write a conclusion that shows that Obi-Wan, Anakin, and Padmé are heroes.

_____

_____

_____

Protecting Padmé

Finish the graphic novel story about Obi-Wan, Anakin, and Padmé. Include words and illustrations. The last box should be the conclusion.

The unknown attacker escaped in a *Koro-2* speeder, but Obi-Wan and Anakin sped closely behind.

When Padmé was attacked in her sleep, Obi-Wan and Anakin were there to protect her.

When the speeder crashed, the unknown attacker ran away through the crowds.

My Character

Imagine a brand-new alien creature or species. Draw a picture here.

Complete the sentences from the point of view of your new character.

My name is _____

I love _____

I really want to _____

I'm afraid of _____

I spend my days _____

My best friend is _____

My family is _____

I am bad at _____

I am great at _____

My Planet

Imagine a brand-new planet.
Draw a picture here.

Answer the questions about
your new planet.

What is the name of the planet?

_____

How many moons and suns does it have?

_____

_____

What is the weather like?

_____

_____

How would you describe the ecosystem (desert, forest, grassland, wetland, marine, or arctic)?

_____

_____

Who lives on your planet?

_____

_____

What is dangerous about your planet?

_____

_____

What is fun about your planet?

_____

_____

My Story Plan

Imagine a story using
your own character and planet.

How does the story start?

_____

_____

_____

What is the problem that your character faces?

_____

_____

_____

What is the solution?

_____

_____

_____

Is there a moral to your story? If so, what is it?

_____

_____

_____

Write your story using your made-up character and planet.
Establish a situation and explain how the action unfolds.
Use dialogue and description along the way.
And don't forget a conclusion!

A long time ago in another galaxy far, far away . . .

_____

_____

_____

_____

_____

_____

_____

_____

_____

_____

_____

_____

Answers

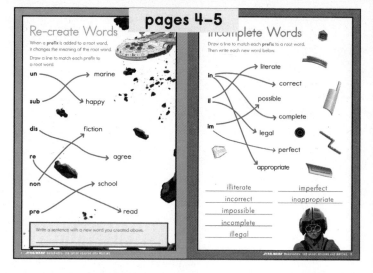

Re-create Words

When a **prefix** is added to a root word, it changes the meaning of the root word.

Draw a line to match each prefix to a root word.

- un → marine
- sub → happy
- dis → fiction
- re → agree
- non → school
- pre → read

Write a sentence with a new word you created above.

Incomplete Words

Draw a line to match each **prefix** to a root word. Then write each new word below.

- in → literate
- il → correct
- im → possible
- → complete
- → legal
- → perfect
- → appropriate

illiterate   imperfect
incorrect   inappropriate
impossible
incomplete
illegal

Resisting Bravely

A **suffix** is added to the end of a root word to change its meaning. Read the definition and example for each suffix. Then write the correct word with its suffix for each definition.

| -y having chill, chilly | -ness state of being happy, happiness | -able can be done understand, understandable | -ly in this way quick, quickly |

- state of being **wicked** — wickedness
- in a **brave** way — bravely
- having **clouds** — cloudy
- state of being **serious** — seriousness
- having **fog** — foggy
- can be **built** — buildable
- can be **flown** — flyable
- in a **wise** way — wisely

Wordy Droids

Write four words you know that contain each suffix.

- -ly
- -y
- -ness
- -able

Decode Words

Circle the root word. Then add the prefix or suffix to it. Write the new word two times.

swamp + y	swampy	swampy
in + put	input	input
orbit + ing	orbiting	orbiting
dis + trust	distrust	distrust
fight + er	fighter	fighter
pre + plan	preplan	preplan
hope + ful	hopeful	hopeful
tele + scope	telescope	telescope
farm + er	farmer	farmer
dis + able	disable	disable

Scavenger Rey

Underline the **prefix** or **suffix** of each word below. Then find the words in the word search.

helpful   fearless   dishonest   unknown
rebuild   defender   forceful   mislead

Write the words in alphabetical order:

defender   dishonest   fearless
forceful   helpful   mislead
rebuild   unknown

Deserted in the Desert

Homographs are words that are spelled alike but mean different things. They may also have different pronunciations.

Choose the correct meaning for each homograph.

Luke lived in the **desert** of Tatooine.
- ☑ a. desert (noun): an ecosystem with little rainfall
- ☐ b. desert (verb): to leave someone behind who needs help

Padmé's royal demeanor and style **entrance** the people of Naboo.
- ☐ a. entrance (noun): the place where one enters or exits
- ☑ b. entrance (verb): to hold one's attention or to fill with wonder

Watto **moped** after losing his slave Anakin in a bet.
- ☑ a. moped (verb): acted sad and hopeless
- ☐ b. moped (noun): a small motorcycle

In most cases, Bail Organa will **object** to war.
- ☐ a. object (noun): something that can be seen or touched
- ☑ b. object (verb): to state one's disagreement

The rebels had a **minute** chance of escaping the Death Star.
- ☐ a. minute (noun): the period of time that takes up 60 seconds
- ☑ b. minute (adjective): very small

As Finn trekked across the snow, his toes grew **number**.
- ☐ a. number (noun): a word or symbol representing a certain amount
- ☑ b. number (adjective): more numb

Write a sentence that includes each homograph, using either meaning.

desert
entrance
moped
object
minute
number

Capital City

A **noun** describes a person, place, or thing. **Proper nouns** name specific people, places, and things and begin with a capital letter.

Circle the proper noun in each pair. Rewrite it with correct capitalization.

planet	lothal	Lothal
warrior	ahsoka tano	Ahsoka Tano
r2-d2	droid	R2-D2
cad bane	bounty hunter	Cad Bane
leader	count dooku	Count Dooku
chewbacca	copilot	Chewbacca
teacher	obi-wan kenobi	Obi-Wan Kenobi
hero	anakin skywalker	Anakin Skywalker
captain rex	clone trooper	Captain Rex

Titles are a word or words that describe a person's job. Titles appear before a person's name. They begin with a capital letter.

Rewrite each sentence using correct capitalization for titles and other proper nouns.

padmé was elected queen amidala at age fourteen.
Padmé was elected Queen Amidala at age fourteen.

anakin skywalker met padmé when she was disguised as a handmaiden.
Anakin Skywalker met Padmé when she was disguised as a handmaiden.

At the time, anakin and his mother, shmi, were slaves on tatooine.
At the time, Anakin and his mother, Shmi, were slaves on Tatooine.

Later, anakin and padmé got married.
Later, Anakin and Padmé got married.

r2-d2 and c-3po were wedding guests.
R2-D2 and C-3PO were wedding guests.

padmé had twins, luke and leia.
Padmé had twins, Luke and Leia.

luke and leia were hidden from emperor palpatine.
Luke and Leia were hidden from Emperor Palpatine.

luke skywalker was raised by his aunt and uncle on tatooine.
Luke Skywalker was raised by his aunt and uncle on Tatooine.

Like Luke

The words below have the same vowel sound as Luke.

Naboo   stormtrooper   dune   grew   Chewbacca
duke   Tatooine   boot   flew   Dooku   fluke

Sort the words by spelling pattern in the boxes below.

ew	oo	u_e
grew	Naboo	dune
Chewbacca	stormtrooper	duke
flew	Tatooine	fluke
	boot	
	Dooku	

Sentient Sentence

A sentence must end with a **period, question mark,** or **exclamation mark.** Add the correct punctuation mark to the end of each sentence.

Admiral Ackbar was a military commander for the Rebel Alliance.

Did you know that he led major operations against the Empire?

Ackbar planned a surprise attack on the second Death Star.

Can you believe that he used construction plans collected by rebel spies?

Ackbar worked with General Calrissian to lead the space battle.

He led from his ship, the Mon Calamari cruiser Home One.

When the battle did not go as planned, he shouted, "It's a trap!"

Ackbar thought the troops needed to retreat right away.

But General Calrissian convinced him to keep going.

The rebels won and destroyed the Death Star!

Roll the Credits

A **comma** is needed between items in a list, a city and a state, and a date and year. Add commas where they are needed in each sentence.

George Lucas founded Lucasfilm in San Rafael, California.

The first Star Wars movie was released May 25, 1977.

It introduced the characters Luke Skywalker, Princess Leia, Han Solo, and Chewbacca.

The movies in the first trilogy were A New Hope, The Empire Strikes Back, and Return of the Jedi.

The prequel trilogy included The Phantom Menace, Attack of the Clones, and Revenge of the Sith.

Lucasfilm headquarters are now in San Francisco, California. Star Wars: The Force Awakens was released December 18, 2015.

New characters include Rey, Finn, Poe, Kylo Ren, and BB-8.

Settings include Takodana, Starkiller Base, and the desert planet Jakku.

Luke's Lightsaber

Possessive form shows that an item belongs to someone, something, or a group.

Write whose items appear in these pictures with the correct punctuation.

Chief Jawa's ion blaster

Darth Vader's TIE fighter

Tusken Raider's gaffi stick

Greedo's blaster

Obi-Wan Kenobi's lightsaber

R5-D4's tread leg

Luke's X-wing starfighter

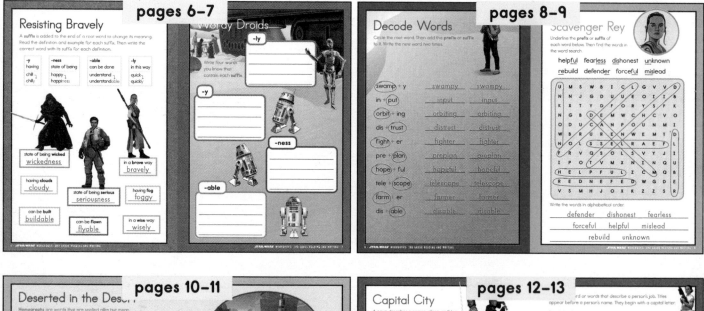

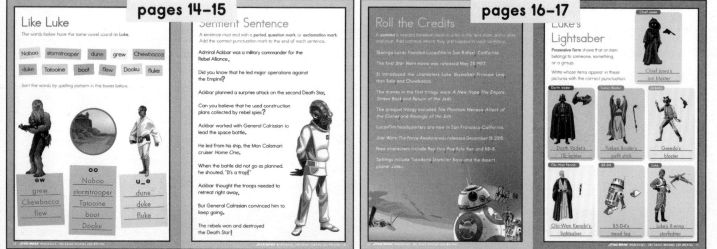

pages 18–19

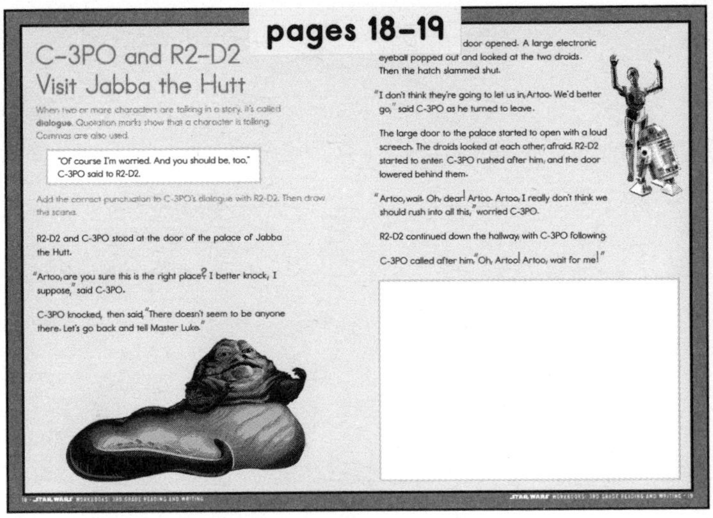
C-3PO and R2-D2 Visit Jabba the Hutt

When two or more characters are talking in a story, it's called **dialogue**. Quotation marks show what a character is talking. Commas are also used.

"Of course I'm worried. And you should be, too," C-3PO said to R2-D2.

Add the correct punctuation to C-3PO's dialogue with R2-D2. Then draw the scene.

R2-D2 and C-3PO stood at the door of the palace of Jabba the Hutt.

"Artoo, are you sure this is the right place? I better knock, I suppose," said C-3PO.

C-3PO knocked, then said, "There doesn't seem to be anyone there. Let's go back and tell Master Luke."

... door opened. A large electronic eyeball popped out and looked at the two droids. Then the hatch slammed shut.

"I don't think they're going to let us in, Artoo. We'd better go," said C-3PO as he turned to leave.

The large door to the palace started to open with a loud screech. The droids looked at each other, afraid. R2-D2 started to enter. C-3PO rushed after him, and the door lowered behind them.

"Artoo, wait. Oh, dear! Artoo. Artoo, I really don't think we should rush into all this," worried C-3PO.

R2-D2 continued down the hallway, with C-3PO following.

C-3PO called after him, "Oh, Artoo! Artoo, wait for me!"

pages 20–21

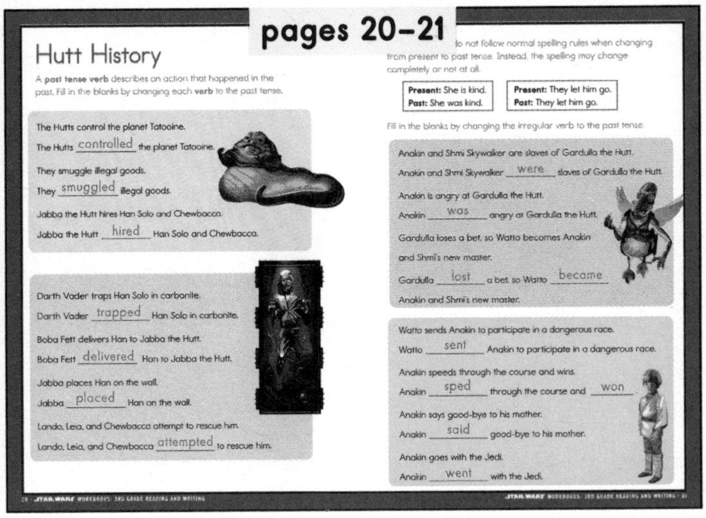
Hutt History

A **past tense verb** describes an action that happened in the past. Fill in the blanks by changing each **verb** to the past tense.

The Hutts control the planet Tatooine.
The Hutts controlled the planet Tatooine.

They smuggle illegal goods.
They smuggled illegal goods.

Jabba the Hutt hires Han Solo and Chewbacca.
Jabba the Hutt hired Han Solo and Chewbacca.

Darth Vader traps Han Solo in carbonite.
Darth Vader trapped Han Solo in carbonite.

Boba Fett delivers Han to Jabba the Hutt.
Boba Fett delivered Han to Jabba the Hutt.

Jabba places Han on the wall.
Jabba placed Han on the wall.

Lando, Leia, and Chewbacca attempt to rescue him.
Lando, Leia, and Chewbacca attempted to rescue him.

... do not follow normal spelling rules when changing from present to past tense. Instead, the spelling may change completely or not at all.

Present: She is kind. **Past:** She was kind.

Present: They let him go. **Past:** They let him go.

Fill in the blanks by changing the irregular verb to the past tense.

Anakin and Shmi Skywalker are slaves of Gardulla the Hutt.
Anakin and Shmi Skywalker were slaves of Gardulla the Hutt.

Anakin is angry at Gardulla the Hutt.
Anakin was angry at Gardulla the Hutt.

Gardulla loses a bet, so Watto becomes Anakin and Shmi's new master.
Gardulla lost a bet, so Watto became Anakin and Shmi's new master.

Watto sends Anakin to participate in a dangerous race.
Watto sent Anakin to participate in a dangerous race.

Anakin speeds through the course and wins.
Anakin sped through the course and won.

Anakin says good-bye to his mother.
Anakin said good-bye to his mother.

Anakin goes with the Jedi.
Anakin went with the Jedi.

pages 22–23

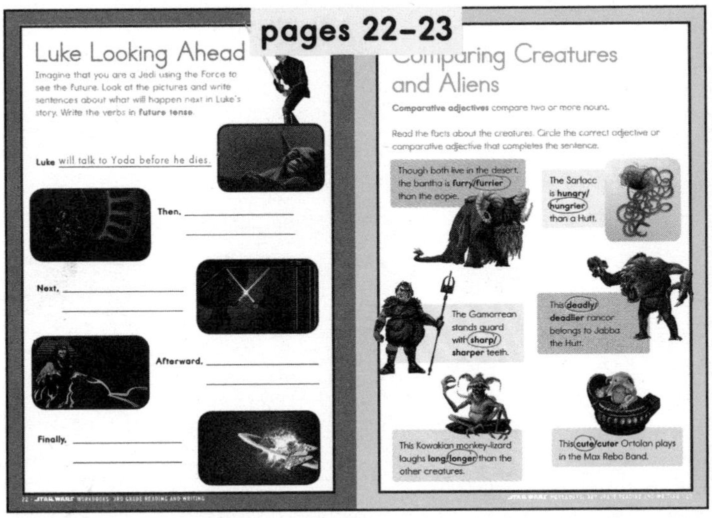
Luke Looking Ahead

Imagine that you are a Jedi using the Force to see the future. Look at the pictures and write sentences about what will happen next in Luke's story. Write the verbs in **future tense**.

Luke will talk to Yoda before he dies.

Then, ______

Next, ______

Afterward, ______

Finally, ______

Comparing Creatures and Aliens

Comparative adjectives compare two or more nouns.

Read the facts about the creatures. Circle the correct adjective or comparative adjective that completes the sentence.

Though both live in the desert, the bantha is furry/(furrier) than the eopie.

The Sarlacc is hungry/(hungrier) than a Hutt.

The Gamorrean stands guard with (sharp)/sharper teeth.

This (deadly)/deadlier rancor belongs to Jabba the Hutt.

This Kowakian monkey-lizard laughs long/(longer) than the other creatures.

This (cute)/cuter Ortolan plays in the Max Rebo Band.

pages 24–25

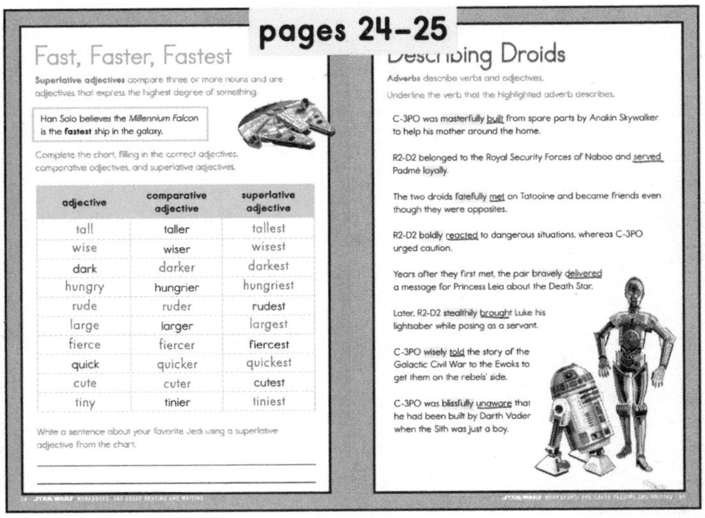
Fast, Faster, Fastest

Superlative adjectives compare three or more nouns and are adjectives that express the highest degree of something.

Han Solo believes the *Millennium Falcon* is the **fastest** ship in the galaxy.

Complete the chart, filling in the correct adjectives, comparative adjectives, and superlative adjectives.

adjective	comparative adjective	superlative adjective
tall	taller	tallest
wise	wiser	wisest
dark	darker	darkest
hungry	hungrier	hungriest
rude	ruder	rudest
large	larger	largest
fierce	fiercer	fiercest
quick	quicker	quickest
cute	cuter	cutest
tiny	tinier	tiniest

Write a sentence about your favorite Jedi using a superlative adjective from the chart.

Describing Droids

Adverbs describe verbs and adjectives.

Underline the verb that the highlighted adverb describes.

C-3PO was masterfully built from spare parts by Anakin Skywalker to help his mother around the home.

R2-D2 belonged to the Royal Security Forces of Naboo and served Padmé loyally.

The two droids fatefully met on Tatooine and became friends even though they were opposites.

R2-D2 boldly reacted to dangerous situations, whereas C-3PO urged caution.

Years after they first met, the pair bravely delivered a message for Princess Leia about the Death Star.

Later, R2-D2 stealthily brought Luke his lightsaber while posing as a servant.

C-3PO wisely told the story of the Galactic Civil War to the Ewoks to get them on the rebels' side.

C-3PO was blissfully unaware that he had been built by Darth Vader when the Sith was just a boy.

pages 26–27

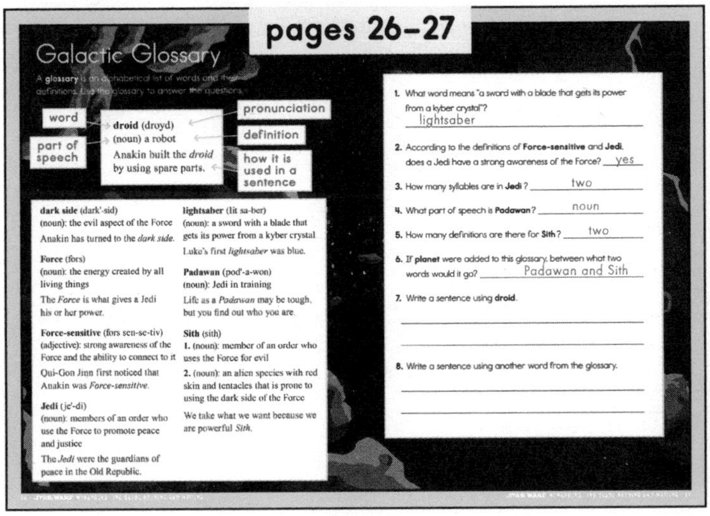
Galactic Glossary

A **glossary** is an alphabetical list of words and their definitions. Use this glossary to answer the questions.

word | pronunciation | part of speech | definition | how it is used in a sentence

droid (droyd) (noun) a robot — Anakin built the *droid* by using spare parts.

dark side (dark'-sid) (noun): the evil aspect of the Force — Anakin has turned to the *dark side*.

Force (fors) (noun): the energy created by all living things — The *Force* is what gives a Jedi his or her power.

Force-sensitive (fors sen-se-tiv) (adjective): strong awareness of the Force and the ability to connect to it — Qui-Gon Jinn first noticed that Anakin was *Force-sensitive*.

Jedi (je'-di) (noun): members of an order who use the Force to promote peace and justice — The *Jedi* were the guardians of peace in the Old Republic.

lightsaber (lit sa-ber) (noun): a sword with a blade that gets its power from a kyber crystal — Luke's first *lightsaber* was blue.

Padawan (pod'-a-won) (noun): Jedi in training — Life as a *Padawan* may be tough, but you find out who you are.

Sith (sith) 1. (noun): member of an order who uses the Force for evil 2. (noun): an alien species with red skin and tentacles that is prone to using the dark side of the Force — We take what we want because we are powerful *Sith*.

1. What word means "a sword with a blade that gets its power from a kyber crystal"? lightsaber
2. According to the definitions of **Force-sensitive** and **Jedi**, does a Jedi have a strong awareness of the Force? yes
3. How many syllables are in **Jedi**? two
4. What part of speech is **Padawan**? noun
5. How many definitions are there for **Sith**? two
6. If **planet** were added to this glossary, between what two words would it go? Padawan and Sith
7. Write a sentence using **droid**.
8. Write a sentence using another word from the glossary.

pages 28–29

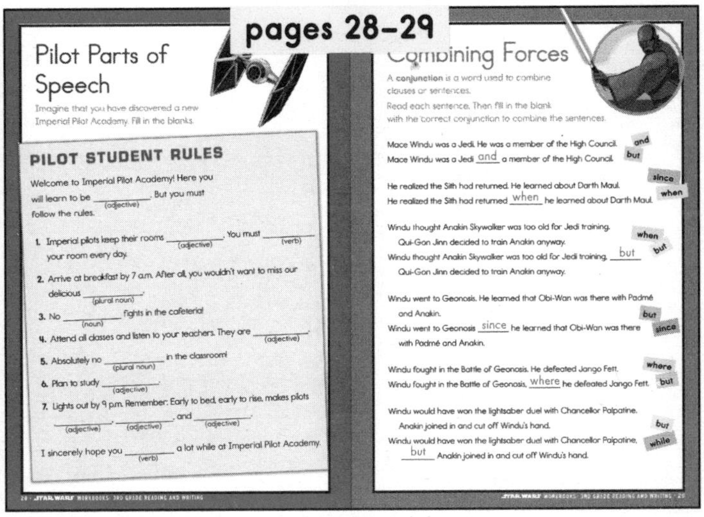
Pilot Parts of Speech

Imagine that you have discovered a new Imperial Pilot Academy. Fill in the blanks.

PILOT STUDENT RULES

Welcome to Imperial Pilot Academy! Here you will learn to be ______ (adjective). But you must follow the rules.

1. Imperial pilots keep their rooms ______ (adjective). You must ______ (verb) your room every day.
2. Arrive at breakfast by 7 a.m. After all, you wouldn't want to miss our delicious ______ (plural noun).
3. No ______ (noun) fights in the cafeteria!
4. Attend all classes and listen to your teachers. They are ______ (adjective).
5. Absolutely no ______ (plural noun) in the classroom!
6. Plan to study ______ (adjective).
7. Lights out by 9 p.m. Remember: Early to bed, early to rise, makes pilots ______ (adjective), ______ (adjective), and ______ (adjective).

I sincerely hope you ______ (verb) a lot while at Imperial Pilot Academy.

Combining Forces

A **conjunction** is a word used to combine clauses or sentences.

Read each sentence. Then fill in the blank with the correct conjunction to combine the sentences.

Mace Windu was a Jedi. He was a member of the High Council.
Mace Windu was a Jedi and a member of the High Council. (and / but)

He realized the Sith had returned. He learned about Darth Maul.
He realized the Sith had returned when he learned about Darth Maul. (since / when)

Windu thought Anakin Skywalker was too old for Jedi training. Qui-Gon Jinn decided to train Anakin anyway.
Windu thought Anakin Skywalker was too old for Jedi training, but Qui-Gon Jinn decided to train Anakin anyway. (when / but)

Windu went to Geonosis. He learned that Obi-Wan was there with Padmé and Anakin.
Windu went to Geonosis since he learned that Obi-Wan was there with Padmé and Anakin. (but / since)

Windu fought in the Battle of Geonosis. He defeated Jango Fett.
Windu fought in the Battle of Geonosis, where he defeated Jango Fett. (where / but)

Windu would have won the lightsaber duel with Chancellor Palpatine. Anakin joined in and cut off Windu's hand.
Windu would have won the lightsaber duel with Chancellor Palpatine, but Anakin joined in and cut off Windu's hand. (but / while)

pages 30–31

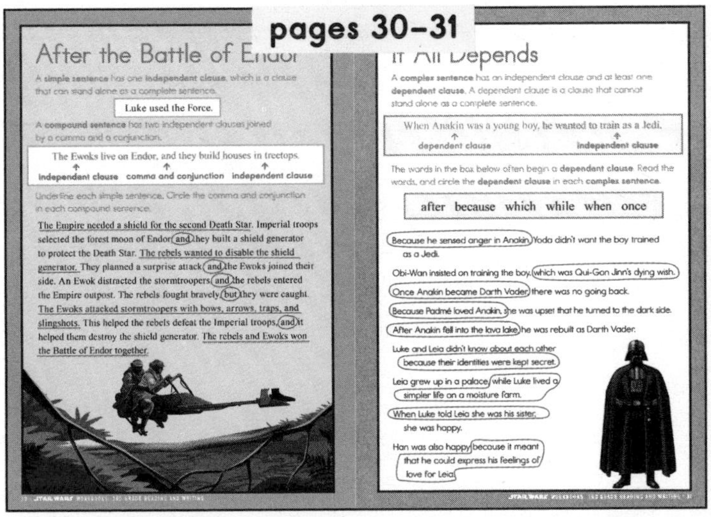
After the Battle of Endor

A **simple sentence** has one **independent clause**, which is a clause that can stand alone as a complete sentence.

Luke used the Force.

A **compound sentence** has two independent clauses joined by a comma and a conjunction.

The Ewoks live on Endor, and they build houses in treetops.
independent clause — comma and conjunction — independent clause

Underline each simple sentence. Circle the comma and conjunction in each compound sentence.

The Empire needed a shield for the second Death Star. Imperial troops selected the forest moon of Endor, (and) they built a shield generator to protect the Death Star. The rebels wanted to disable the shield generator. They planned a surprise attack, (and) the Ewoks joined their side. An Ewok distracted the stormtroopers, (and) the rebels entered the Empire outpost. The rebels fought bravely, (but) they were caught. The Ewoks attacked stormtroopers with bows, arrows, traps, and slingshots. This helped the rebels defeat the Imperial troops, (and) it helped them destroy the shield generator. The rebels and Ewoks won the Battle of Endor together.

It All Depends

A **complex sentence** has an independent clause and at least one **dependent clause**. A dependent clause is a clause that cannot stand alone as a complete sentence.

When Anakin was a young boy, he wanted to train as a Jedi.
dependent clause — independent clause

The words in the box below often begin a **dependent clause**. Read the words, and circle the **dependent clause** in each **complex sentence**.

after because which while when once

(Because he sensed anger in Anakin,) Yoda didn't want the boy trained as a Jedi.

Obi-Wan insisted on training the boy, (which was Qui-Gon Jinn's dying wish.)

(Once Anakin became Darth Vader,) there was no going back.

(Because Padmé loved Anakin,) she was upset that he turned to the dark side.

(After Anakin fell into the lava lake,) he was rebuilt as Darth Vader.

Luke and Leia didn't know about each other (because their identities were kept secret.)

Leia grew up in a palace, (while Luke lived a simpler life on a moisture farm.)

(When Luke told Leia she was his sister,) she was happy.

Han was also happy (because it meant that he could express his feelings of love for Leia.)

pages 32–33

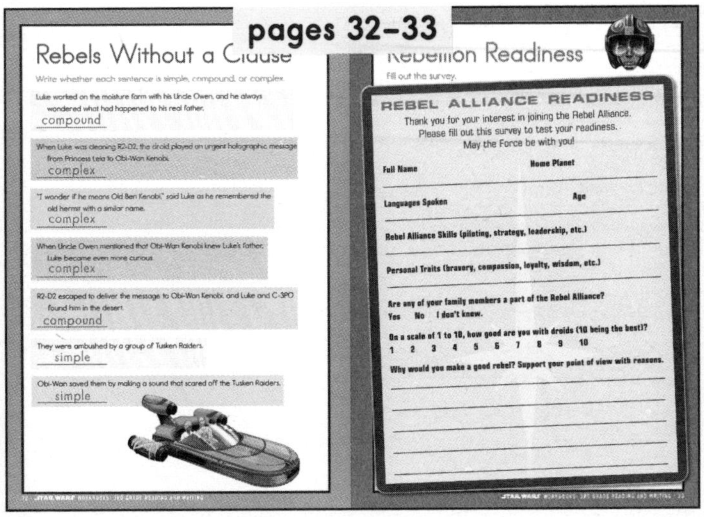
Rebels Without a Clause

Write whether each sentence is simple, compound, or complex.

Luke worked on the moisture farm with his Uncle Owen, and he always wondered what had happened to his real father. compound

When Luke was cleaning R2-D2, the droid played an urgent holographic message from Princess Leia to Obi-Wan Kenobi. complex

"I wonder if he means Old Ben Kenobi," said Luke as he remembered the old hermit with a similar name. complex

When Uncle Owen mentioned that Obi-Wan Kenobi knew Luke's father, Luke became even more curious. complex

R2-D2 escaped to deliver the message to Obi-Wan Kenobi, and Luke and C-3PO found him in the desert. compound

They were ambushed by a group of Tusken Raiders. simple

Obi-Wan saved them by making a sound that scared off the Tusken Raiders. simple

Rebellion Readiness

Fill out the survey.

REBEL ALLIANCE READINESS

Thank you for your interest in joining the Rebel Alliance. Please fill out this survey to test your readiness. May the Force be with you!

Full Name | Home Planet

Languages Spoken | Age

Rebel Alliance Skills (piloting, strategy, leadership, etc.)

Personal Traits (bravery, compassion, loyalty, wisdom, etc.)

Are any of your family members a part of the Rebel Alliance? Yes No I don't know.

On a scale of 1 to 10, how good are you with droids (10 being the best!)? 1 2 3 4 5 6 7 8 9 10

Why would you make a good rebel? Support your point of view with reasons.

Answers

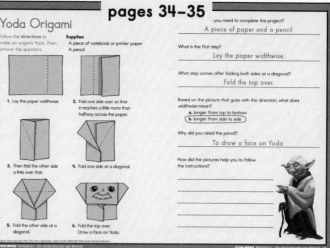

pages 34–35

Yoda Origami

Follow the directions to make an origami Yoda. Then answer the questions.

Supplies:
A piece of notebook or printer paper
A pencil

1. Lay the paper widthwise.
2. Fold one side over so that it reaches a little more than halfway across the paper.
3. Then fold the other side a little over that.
4. Fold one side at a diagonal.
5. Fold the other side at a diagonal.
6. Fold the top over. Draw a face on Yoda.

...you need to complete this project?
A piece of paper and a pencil

What is the first step?
Lay the paper widthwise.

What step comes after folding both sides at a diagonal?
Fold the top over.

Based on the picture that goes with the direction, what does widthwise mean?
a. longer from top to bottom
b. longer from side to side

Why did you need the pencil?
To draw a face on Yoda

How did the pictures help you to follow the instructions?

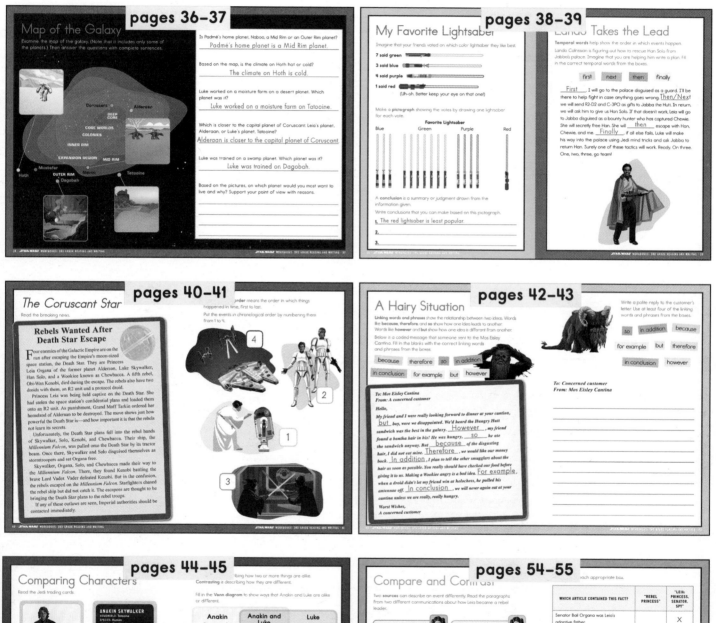

pages 36–37

Map of the Galaxy

Examine the map of the galaxy. (Note that it includes only some of the planets.) Then answer the questions with complete sentences.

Is Padmé's home planet, Naboo, a Mid Rim or an Outer Rim planet?
Padmé's home planet is a Mid Rim planet.

Based on the map, is the climate on Hoth hot or cold?
The climate on Hoth is cold.

Luke worked on a moisture farm on a desert planet. Which planet was it?
Luke worked on a moisture farm on Tatooine.

Which is closer to the capital planet of Coruscant: Leia's planet, Alderaan, or Luke's planet, Tatooine?
Alderaan is closer to the capital planet of Coruscant.

Luke was trained on a swamp planet. Which planet was it?
Luke was trained on Dagobah.

Based on the pictures, on which planet would you most want to live and why? Support your point of view with reasons.

pages 38–39

My Favorite Lightsaber

Imagine that your friends voted on which color lightsaber they like best.

7 said green
3 said blue
4 said purple
1 said red
(Uh-oh. Better keep your eye on that one!)

Make a **pictograph** showing the votes by drawing one lightsaber for each vote.

Favorite Lightsaber
Blue · Green · Purple · Red

A **conclusion** is a summary or judgment drawn from the information given.

Write conclusions that you can make based on this pictograph.

1. **The red lightsaber is least popular.**
2.
3.

Lando Takes the Lead

Temporal words help show the order in which events happen. Lando Calrissian is figuring out how to rescue Han Solo from Jabba's palace. Imagine that you are helping him write a plan. Fill in the correct temporal words from the boxes.

first   next   then   finally

First, I will go to the palace disguised as a guard. I'll be there to help fight in case anything goes wrong. **Then/Next** we will send R2-D2 and C-3PO as gifts to Jabba the Hutt. In return, we will ask him to give up Han Solo. If that doesn't work, Lando will go to Jabba disguised as a bounty hunter who has captured Chewie. She will secretly free Han. She will **then** escape with Han, Chewie, and me. **Finally**, if all else fails, Luke will make his way into the palace using Jedi mind tricks and ask Jabba to return Han. Surely one of these tactics will work. Ready. On three. One, two, three, go team!

pages 40–41

The Coruscant Star

Read the breaking news.

Rebels Wanted After Death Star Escape

Four enemies of the Galactic Empire are on the run after escaping the Empire's moon-sized space station, the Death Star. They are Princess Leia Organa of the former planet Alderaan, Luke Skywalker, Han Solo, and a Wookiee known as Chewbacca. A fifth rebel, Obi-Wan Kenobi, died during the escape. The rebels also have two droids with them, an R2 unit and a protocol droid.

Princess Leia was being held captive on the Death Star. She had stolen the space station's confidential plans and loaded them onto an R2 unit. As punishment, Grand Moff Tarkin ordered her homeland of Alderaan to be destroyed. The move shows just how powerful the Death Star is—and how important it is that the rebels not learn its secrets.

Unfortunately, the Death Star plans fell into the rebel hands of Skywalker, Solo, Kenobi, and Chewbacca. Their ship, the Millennium Falcon, was pulled onto the Death Star by its tractor beam. Once there, Skywalker and Solo disguised themselves as stormtroopers and set Organa free.

Skywalker, Organa, Solo, and Chewbacca made their way to the Millennium Falcon. There, they found Kenobi battling the brave Lord Vader. Vader defeated Kenobi. But in the confusion, the rebels escaped on the Millennium Falcon. Starfighters chased the rebel ship but did not catch it. The escapees are thought to be bringing the Death Star plans to the rebel troops.

If any of these outlaws are seen, Imperial authorities should be contacted immediately.

...order means the order in which things happened in time, first to last.

Put the events in chronological order by numbering them from 1 to 4.

4 · 2 · 1 · 3

pages 42–43

A Hairy Situation

Linking words and phrases show the relationship between two ideas. Words like **because**, **therefore**, and **so** show how one idea leads to another. Words like **however** and **but** show how one idea is different from another.

Below is a coded message that someone sent to the Mos Eisley Cantina. Fill in the blanks with the correct linking words and phrases from the boxes.

because · therefore · so · in addition
in conclusion · for example · but · however

To: Mos Eisley Cantina
From: A concerned customer

Hello,

My friend and I were really looking forward to dinner at your cantina, **but** boy, were we disappointed. We'd heard the Hungry Hutt sandwich was the best in the galaxy. **However**, my friend found a bantha hair in his! He was hungry, **so** he ate the sandwich anyway. But **because** of the disgusting hair, I did not eat mine. **Therefore**, we would like our money back. **In addition**, I plan to tell the other smugglers about how hairy your food is. You really should have checked our food before giving it to us. Making a Wookiee angry is a bad idea. **For example**, when a droid didn't let my friend win at holochess, he pulled his antennae off. **In conclusion**, we will never again eat at your cantina unless we are really, really hungry.

Worst Wishes,
A concerned customer

Write a polite reply to the customer's letter. Use at least four of the linking words and phrases from the boxes.

so · in addition · because
for example · but · therefore
in conclusion · however

To: Concerned customer
From: Mos Eisley Cantina

pages 44–45

Comparing Characters

Read the Jedi trading cards.

ANAKIN SKYWALKER
HOMEWORLD: Tatooine
SPECIES: Human
MENTOR: Obi-Wan Kenobi
LIGHTSABER COLOR: blue

LUKE SKYWALKER
HOMEWORLD: Tatooine
SPECIES: Human
MENTOR: Obi-Wan Kenobi
LIGHTSABER COLOR: First blue, then green

...bing how two or more things are alike.
Contrasting is describing how they are different.

Fill in the **Venn diagram** to show ways that Anakin and Luke are alike or different.

Anakin	Anakin and Luke	Luke
Discovered at age nine	Both Force-sensitive	Discovered at age nineteen
Turned to the dark side	Obi-Wan Kenobi was their mentor	Did not turn to the dark side
Did not use a green lightsaber	Both used blue lightsabers	Used a green lightsaber
Earned a nickname during the Clone Wars	Both are human	Did not earn a nickname during the Clone Wars
Was a slave	Both are from Tatooine	Was never a slave

Use your Venn diagram to write a paragraph that compares and contrasts Anakin and Luke. Include one linking word from the boxes below in each sentence.

also · another · and · more · but

pages 54–55

Compare and Contrast

Two **sources** can describe an event differently. Read the paragraphs from two different communications about how Leia became a rebel leader.

REBEL PRINCESS

How did a wealthy princess become a great rebel leader? For one thing, Leia, Princess of Alderaan, was no ordinary princess. She was the youngest Senator elected to the Imperial Senate, and fearlessly fought against the evil Empire.

With the Force strong in Leia, she was destined to bring order to the galaxy. Leia also inherited her birth mother Padmé's leadership abilities. As Senator, she criticized the Emperor's unjust rule. Meanwhile, she visited other planets to help people hurt by the Empire. Her courage and dedication helped lead to the Death Star's destruction, a turning point in the revolution. As a leader of the Rebellion, victory would be hers.

LEIA: PRINCESS, SENATOR, SPY

Leia's peaceful childhood on Alderaan made her an unlikely rebel leader. But actually, Leia was following in her father's footsteps. Bail Organa, Leia's adoptive father, was a Senator who worked side by side with Emperor Palpatine. However, Bail secretly planned to overthrow the Empire when the time was right. Leia, too, would fight Emperor Palpatine from inside the Senate.

At the early age of eighteen, she was elected Senator of Alderaan and accomplished a lot in her youth. As Senator, she criticized the Emperor for his unjust rule. Meanwhile, she helped build the Rebel Alliance with her father. After the tragic destruction of Alderaan and death of her father, Leia became an important leader of the Rebellion.

...each appropriate box.

WHICH ARTICLE CONTAINED THIS FACT?	"REBEL PRINCESS"	"LEIA: PRINCESS, SENATOR, SPY"
Senator Bail Organa was Leia's adoptive father.		X
Padmé was Leia's mother.	X	
Leia became Senator at age eighteen.		X
Leia inherited Padmé's leadership skills.	X	
Leia criticized the Emperor.	X	X
Alderaan was destroyed.		X
Leia visited other planets to help people.	X	
Leia was a leader of the Rebellion.	X	X

Both sources state that Leia became Senator, but they suggest that different people influenced her ability to be a strong leader. What does the first article say? What does the second article say?

The first article said that she inherited her leadership abilities from her birth mother, Padmé. The second article said that she was following the example of her adoptive father, Bail Organa.

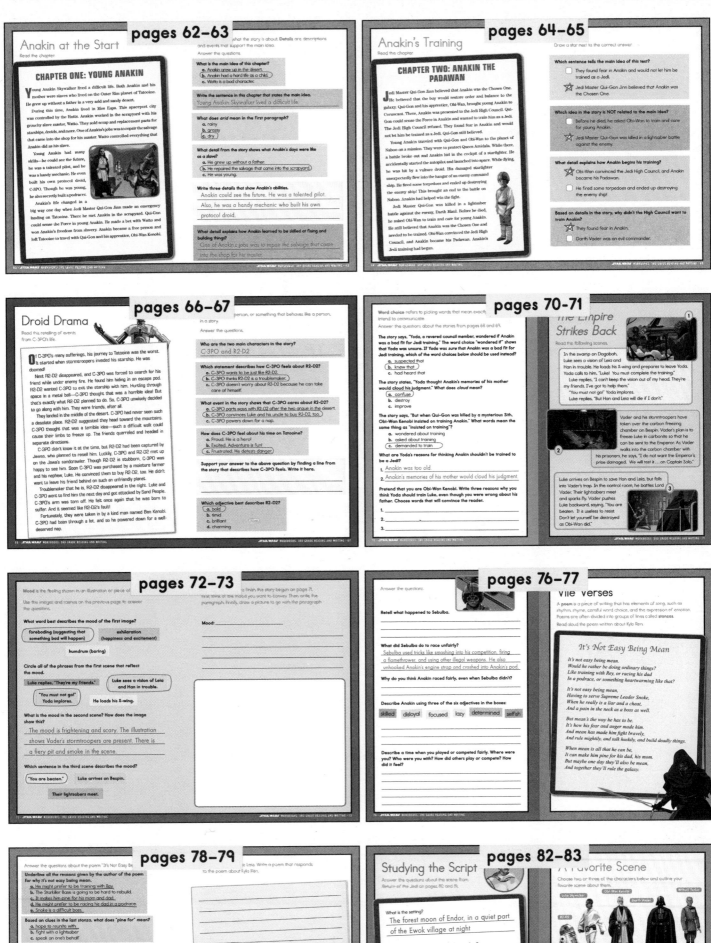

pages 62–63

Anakin at the Start

Read the chapter.

CHAPTER ONE: YOUNG ANAKIN

Young Anakin Skywalker lived a difficult life. Both Anakin and his mother were slaves who lived on the Outer Rim planet of Tatooine. He grew up without a father in a very arid and sandy desert.

During this time, Anakin lived in Mos Espa. This spaceport city was controlled by the Hutts. Anakin worked in the scrapyard with his grouchy slave master, Watto. They sold scrap and replacement parts for starships, droids, and more. One of Anakin's jobs was to repair the salvage that came into the shop for his master. Watto controlled everything that Anakin did as his slave.

Young Anakin had many skills—he could see the future, he was a talented pilot, and he was a handy mechanic. He even built his own protocol droid, C-3PO. Though he was young, he also secretly built a podracer.

Anakin's life changed in a big way one day when Jedi Master Qui-Gon Jinn made an emergency landing on Tatooine. There he met Anakin in the scrapyard. Qui-Gon could sense the Force in young Anakin. He made a bet with Watto and won Anakin's freedom from slavery. Anakin became a free person and left Tatooine to travel with Qui-Gon and his apprentice, Obi-Wan Kenobi.

...what the story is about. Details are descriptions and events that support the main idea.

Answer the questions.

What is the main idea of this chapter?
a. Anakin grew up in the desert.
b. Anakin had a hard life as a child. (circled)
c. Watto is a bad character.

Write the sentence in this chapter that states the main idea.
Young Anakin Skywalker lived a difficult life.

What does *arid* mean in the first paragraph?
a. rainy
b. grassy
c. dry (circled)

What detail from the story shows what Anakin's days were like as a slave?
a. He grew up without a father.
b. He repaired the salvage that came into the scrapyard. (circled)
c. He was young.

Write three details that show Anakin's abilities.
Anakin could see the future. He was a talented pilot. Also, he was a handy mechanic who built his own protocol droid.

What detail explains how Anakin learned to be skilled at fixing and building things?
One of Anakin's jobs was to repair the salvage that came into the shop for his master.

pages 64–65

Anakin's Training

Read the chapter.

CHAPTER TWO: ANAKIN THE PADAWAN

Jedi Master Qui-Gon Jinn believed that Anakin was the Chosen One. He believed that the boy would restore order and balance to the galaxy. Qui-Gon and his apprentice, Obi-Wan, brought young Anakin to Coruscant. There, Anakin was presented to the Jedi High Council. Qui-Gon could sense the Force in Anakin and wanted to train him as a Jedi. The Jedi High Council refused. They found fear in Anakin and would not let him be trained as a Jedi. Qui-Gon still believed.

Young Anakin traveled with Qui-Gon and Obi-Wan to the planet of Naboo on a mission. They were to protect Queen Amidala. While there, a battle broke out and Anakin hid in the cockpit of a starfighter. He accidentally started the autopilot and launched into space. While flying, he was hit by a vulture droid. His damaged starfighter unexpectedly flew into the hangar of an enemy command ship. He fired some torpedoes and ended up destroying the enemy ship! This brought an end to the battle on Naboo. Anakin had helped win the fight.

Jedi Master Qui-Gon was killed in a lightsaber battle against the enemy, Darth Maul. Before he died, he asked Obi-Wan to train and care for young Anakin. He still believed that Anakin was the Chosen One and needed to be trained. Obi-Wan convinced the Jedi High Council, and Anakin became his Padawan. Anakin's Jedi training had begun.

Draw a star next to the correct answer.

Which sentence tells the main idea of this text?
- They found fear in Anakin and would not let him be trained as a Jedi.
- ☆ Jedi Master Qui-Gon Jinn believed that Anakin was the Chosen One.

Which idea in the story is NOT related to the main idea?
- Before he died, he asked Obi-Wan to train and care for young Anakin.
- ☆ Jedi Master Qui-Gon was killed in a lightsaber battle against the enemy.

What detail explains how Anakin begins his training?
- ☆ Obi-Wan convinced the Jedi High Council, and Anakin became his Padawan.
- He fired some torpedoes and ended up destroying the enemy ship!

Based on details in the story, why didn't the High Council want to train Anakin?
- ☆ They found fear in Anakin.
- Darth Vader was an evil commander.

pages 66–67

Droid Drama

Read this retelling of events from C-3PO's life.

Of C-3PO's many sufferings, his journey to Tatooine was the worst. It started when stormtroopers invaded his starship. He was doomed!

Next R2-D2 disappeared, and C-3PO was forced to search for his friend while under enemy fire. He found him hiding in an escape pod. R2-D2 wanted C-3PO to exit the starship with him. Hurtling through space in a metal ball—C-3PO thought that was a horrible idea! But that's exactly what R2-D2 planned to do. So, C-3PO unwisely decided to go along with him. They were friends, after all.

They landed in the middle of the desert. C-3PO had never seen such a desolate place. R2-D2 suggested they head toward the mountains. C-3PO thought that was a terrible idea—such a difficult walk could cause their limbs to freeze up. The friends quarreled and headed in separate directions.

C-3PO didn't know it at the time, but R2-D2 had been captured by Jawas, who planned to resell him. Luckily, C-3PO and R2-D2 met up on the Jawa's sandcrawler. Though R2-D2 is stubborn, C-3PO was happy to see him. Soon C-3PO was purchased by a moisture farmer and his nephew, Luke. He convinced them to buy R2-D2, too. He didn't want to leave his friend behind on such an unfriendly planet.

Troublemaker that he is, R2-D2 disappeared in the night. Luke and C-3PO went to find him the next day and got attacked by Sand People. C-3PO's arm was torn off. He felt once again that he was born to suffer. And it seemed like R2-D2's fault!

Fortunately, they were taken in by a kind man named Ben Kenobi. C-3PO had been through a lot, and so he powered down for a well-deserved nap.

...person, or something that behaves like a person, in a story.

Answer the questions.

Who are the two main characters in the story?
C-3PO and R2-D2

Which statement describes how C-3PO feels about R2-D2?
a. C-3PO wants to be just like R2-D2.
b. C-3PO thinks R2-D2 is a troublemaker. (circled)
c. C-3PO doesn't worry about R2-D2 because he can take care of himself.

What event in the story shows that C-3PO cares about R2-D2?
a. C-3PO parts ways with R2-D2 after the two argue in the desert.
b. C-3PO convinces Luke and his uncle to buy R2-D2, too. (circled)
c. C-3PO powers down for a nap.

How does C-3PO feel about his time on Tatooine?
a. Proud. He is a hero!
b. Excited. Adventure is fun!
c. Frustrated. He detests danger. (circled)

Support your answer to the above question by finding a line from the story that describes how C-3PO feels. Write it here.

Which adjective best describes R2-D2?
a. bold (circled)
b. timid
c. brilliant
d. charming

pages 70–71

Word choice refers to picking words that mean exactly... intend to communicate.

Answer the questions about the stories from pages 68 and 69.

The story says, "Yoda, a revered council member, wondered if Anakin was a bad fit for Jedi training." The word choice "wondered if" shows that Yoda was unsure. If Yoda was *sure* that Anakin was a bad fit for Jedi training, which of the word choices below should be used instead?
a. suspected that
b. knew that (circled)
c. had heard that

The story states, "Yoda thought Anakin's memories of his mother would cloud his judgment." What does *cloud* mean?
a. confuse (circled)
b. destroy
c. improve

The story says, "But when Qui-Gon was killed by a mysterious Sith, Obi-Wan Kenobi insisted on training Anakin." What words mean the same thing as "insisted on training"?
a. wondered about training
b. asked about training
c. demanded to train (circled)

What are Yoda's reasons for thinking Anakin shouldn't be trained to be a Jedi?
1. Anakin was too old.
2. Anakin's memories of his mother would cloud his judgment.

Pretend that you are Obi-Wan Kenobi. Write three reasons why you think Yoda should train Luke, even though you were wrong about his father. Choose words that will convince the reader.
1.
2.
3.

The Empire Strikes Back

Read the following scenes.

1. In the swamp on Dagobah, Luke sees a vision of Leia and Han in trouble. He loads his X-wing and prepares to leave Yoda. Yoda calls to him. "Luke! You must complete the training."
Luke replies, "I can't keep the vision out of my head. They're my friends. I've got to help them."
"You must not go!" Yoda implores.
Luke replies, "But Han and Leia will die if I don't."

2. Vader and his stormtroopers have taken over the carbon freezing chamber on Bespin. Vader's plan is to freeze Luke in carbonite so that he can be sent to the Emperor. As Vader walks into the carbon chamber with his prisoners, he says, "I do not want the Emperor's prize damaged. We will test it . . . on Captain Solo."

3. Luke arrives on Bespin to save Han and Leia, but falls into Vader's trap. In the control room, he battles Lord Vader. Their lightsabers meet and sparks fly. Vader pushes Luke backward, saying, "You are beaten. It is useless to resist. Don't let yourself be destroyed as Obi-Wan did."

pages 72–73

Mood is the feeling shown in an illustration or piece of...

Use the images and scenes on the previous page to answer the questions.

What word best describes the mood of the first image?
- foreboding (suggesting that something bad will happen) (circled)
- exhilaration (happiness and excitement)
- humdrum (boring)

Circle all of the phrases from the first scene that reflect the mood.
- Luke replies, "They're my friends."
- Luke sees a vision of Leia and Han in trouble. (circled)
- "You must not go!" Yoda implores. (circled)
- He loads his X-wing.

What is the mood in the second scene? How does the image show this?
The mood is frightening and scary. The illustration shows Vader's stormtroopers are present. There is a fiery pit and smoke in the scene.

Which sentence in the third scene describes the mood?
- "You are beaten." (circled)
- Luke arrives on Bespin.
- Their lightsabers meet.

...o finish the story begun on page 71. First, think of the mood you want to convey. Then write the paragraph. Finally, draw a picture to go with the paragraph.

Mood:

pages 76–77

Answer the questions.

Retell what happened to Sebulba.

What did Sebulba do to race unfairly?
Sebulba used tricks like smashing into his competition, firing a flamethrower, and using other illegal weapons. He also unhooked Anakin's engine strap and crashed into Anakin's pod.

Why do you think Anakin raced fairly, even when Sebulba didn't?

Describe Anakin using three of the six adjectives in the boxes:
skilled (shaded) | disloyal | focused | lazy | determined (shaded) | selfish

Describe a time when you played or competed fairly. Where were you? Who were you with? How did others play or compete? How did it feel?

Vile Verses

A **poem** is a piece of writing that has elements of song, such as rhythm, rhyme, careful word choice, and the expression of emotion. Poems are often divided into groups of lines called **stanzas**.

Read aloud the poem written about Kylo Ren.

It's Not Easy Being Mean

It's not easy being mean.
Would he rather be doing ordinary things?
Like training with Rey, or racing his dad
In a podrace, or something heartwarming like that?

It's not easy being mean,
Having to serve Supreme Leader Snoke,
When he really is a liar and a cheat,
And a pain in the neck as a boss as well.

But mean's the way he has to be.
It's how his fear and anger made him.
And mean has made him fight bravely,
And rule mightily, and talk huskily, and build deadly things.

When mean is all that he can be,
It can make him pine for his dad, his mom.
But maybe one day they'll also be mean,
And together they'll rule the galaxy.

pages 78–79

Answer the questions about the poem "It's Not Easy Be...

Underline all the reasons given by the author of the poem for why it's not easy being mean.
a. He might prefer to be training with Rey. (underlined)
b. The Starkiller Base is going to be hard to rebuild.
c. It makes him pine for his mom and dad. (underlined)
d. He might prefer to be racing his dad in a podrace. (underlined)
e. Snoke is a difficult boss. (underlined)

Based on clues in the last stanza, what does "pine for" mean?
a. hope to reunite with (underlined)
b. fight with a lightsaber
c. speak on one's behalf

According to the author, in the third stanza, what conclusions can be drawn from the word choices "fight bravely" and "rule mightily"?
a. Kylo Ren is ashamed of himself for being mean.
b. In a way, Kylo Ren is proud of the mean things he does. (underlined)
c. Kylo Ren thinks that being mean is a cowardly decision.

What does "pain in the neck" mean in the second stanza?
a. a hurting neck
b. charming
c. annoying (underlined)

What might Han Solo and Leia say about Kylo Ren's plan to rule the galaxy together?

Circle which statement you agree with.
- It is easier to be nice than it is to be mean.
- It is easier to be mean than it is to be nice.

Write two sentences that support your answer.

...Leia. Write a poem that responds to the poem about Kylo Ren.

pages 82–83

Studying the Script

Answer the questions about the scene from *Return of the Jedi* on pages 80 and 81.

What is the setting?
The forest moon of Endor, in a quiet part of the Ewok village at night

What does Leia remember about her mother?
Images and feelings, that she was very beautiful and kind, but sad

Why must Luke face Vader?
Because Vader is Luke's father.

In this scene, what is the first action described?
Leia moves away from Luke.

What does Leia do when she learns that she is Luke's sister?
She tells Luke that she has always known.

A Favorite Scene

Choose two or three of the characters below and outline your favorite scene about them.

List your characters.

Write what happens.
First,
Next,
Then,
Finally,

What do your characters say to start the scene?